先哲名言

中国先哲文辞精粹

CHINESE MAXIMS

Golden Sayings of Chinese Thinkers Over Five Thousand Years

宫达非　冯　禹　主编

华语教学出版社
北　京

First Edition 1994

Second Printing 1996

ISBN 7-80052-424-8

Published by Sinolingua

24 Baiwanzhuang Road, Beijing 100037, China

Printed by Beijing Foreign Languages Printing House

Distributed by China International

Book Trading Corporation

35 Chegongzhuang Xilu, P.O.Box 399

Beijing 100044, China

Printed in the People's Republic of China

目 录

序

“十年树木，百年树人”。在新掀起的国际产业革命大潮中，世界各国正激烈竞争。如何教育和塑造人，是关系到每个国家成败的头等大事。“优胜劣汰”不仅是自然界，也是国家、民族的发展规律；而决定的因素则是人。

一些世界著名学者在论及现代西方社会时指出：由于高科技的发展，物资生产已极大丰富，而精神文明、社会道德却是江河日下，社会问题恶性爆炸，已成为社会进步的严重障碍。他们呼吁科学教育与道德教育并举，否则人类可能被自己的伟大的科学成就所毁灭。他们还曾经这样提出，“人类想在二十一世纪生存下去，须要到中国孔夫子那里去寻找智慧”。

自六十年代以后，日本和亚洲“四小龙”经济崛起，引起了一些国家以至西方发达国家刮目相视。东亚地区从文化范畴看都属东方文化，具体讲是属于以中国儒家哲学思想为主流的东亚文化，特别是在社会伦理道德方面。尽管学者们对儒学思想对东亚经济发展的影响与作用的问题上还有争议，但这种争议只是就影响与作用的大小和多少而言，而不是完全无视这种影响与作用的存在。

1984 年，日本中曾根康弘首相来华访问同胡耀邦总书记谈话时，曾经这样提到：日本在发展经济的道路上是向欧美借鉴和学习的，在对社会伦理道德教育的问题上，仍然以中国儒家哲学为指导。胡耀邦同志事后谈及此事时说，结合日本实际情况，觉得中曾根的谈话很有道理，值得我们深思。

近年来，中国派很多专家赴日本考察工商管理，日本朋友却说，他们日本的许多管理思想，是从中国学的。例如：有名的“松下电器商学院”商业道德课的读本就是《大学》、《论语》、《孟子》和《孝经》,其学习目标在于:“明明德”、“亲民”、“至善”。

欧美研究日本的一些专家指出,日本在发展现代经济中,其现代性能与传统性很协调地互相结合。日本人热爱工作,吃苦耐劳,重家庭伦理,对人彬彬有礼,强烈地体现他们是具有东方文明的国家。

“四小龙”之一的新加坡,前几年曾根据儒家优秀思想,编写了几种中学课本,对公民从青少年时代起进行伦理道德教育。这对于把新加坡建设成为一个现代化文明国家起了很重要的作用。据美国商业环境风险咨询公司 1991 年的调查,新加坡工人的质量(素质教育、守法观念、工作态度和技术熟练程度)名列世界第一。

工业革命和资本主义兴起以后,西方强国在经济、文化各方面率领世界风骚已达数百年之久。东亚地区经济崛起之后,这种形势已开始有所倾斜了。美国一位有名的政治家甚至这样指出:二十一世纪,将是以中国儒学文化为指导的亚洲太平洋经济圈的时代。当然有些人至今仍认为受儒家文化影响的东亚文化阻碍经济发展,阻碍社会进步,这是一种偏见,在事实面前应该重新反思。

中国传统文化的精华,在一定程度上,可以概括为“民吾同胞,物吾与也”的天人一体思想,追求的是“为天地立心”,“为生民立命”,“为万世开太平”。也就是说,要树立正确的“人生观”、“世界观”、“价值观”。这也可以说是世界文化的精华。就整体而言,中国传统文化也有落后的东西,然而如果把封建社会的糟粕统统归罪于中国传统文化,则是片面的、不实际的。

从八十年代起,在“改革开放”伟大战略决策指引下,在短短的十多年中,我们的国家建设已经发生了重大的、富有新气象的变化,在各个方面取得了巨大成就并已引致举世瞩目。随着经济的发展,特别是计划经济向市场经济转轨,社会道德和精神文明建设,也有所进步,如人际关系已有好转;奋发前进、合理竞争、多劳多得的价值观，已得到社会的公认而逐步实现，重经济、重科学、重知识、重文化已成为社会新风尚。但与此同时，诸种弊端，也应时而生，如拜金主义，以权谋私，见利忘义，伪劣假冒以至偷盗抢劫等，正严重地败坏着社会道德，成为公害。我们已经提出经济建设与精神文明和社会道德教育两手一齐抓，不能偏废。相信在深化改革的实践中，继承发扬传统文化的精华，借鉴和汲取外国特别是发达国家的优秀文化，我们中国特色社会主义的新文化和精神文明一定能逐步建设起来。

我们编辑《先哲名言》这本书，正是为了这一目的，从丰厚的中国哲理文献中，我们选择了部分名言，这些名言，好像随着历史长河飘流的花朵，在人类面前，仍然有她的色、香和真善美的价值，不仅可以增益智慧，而且可以启迪人们如何做一个有价值的真正的人；我们编这本书是为了满足那些追赶时代实行自我终身教育人的需要，是为了满足那些在各条战线紧张拼搏的人、那些善于从古代典籍或是现实生活中吸取营养来完善自己的人的需要，希望这些古代的先哲名言能震荡你的心灵，诱发人们前进的新思。这是我们所企盼的。我们编辑这本书，还同时也是为了给那些试图从中国浩瀚渊博的传统文化中"寻找智慧"的外国人士、专家、学者们提供一些方便，如果能达到这样的目的，我们将感到荣幸和欣慰。

谨此以为序。

宫达非
一九九三年春二月

PREFACE

The cultivation of human beings is of vital importance to any great undertaking. In the face of the surging new industrial revolution and intense worldwide competition, how to educate and mould people may decide the destiny of a nation. The fittest survive, and the weak perish—this applies to nations as well as to nature. Human beings, however, are the decisive factor.

Some scholars of world renown point out that in modern Western societies, material production has greatly expanded thanks to high technology, but ethical standards and social morals have rapidly declined. They note that mounting social problems have seriously impeded the progress of society. They warn that the human race could be destroyed by its own scientific achievements unless moral education and scientific education go hand in hand. They even suggest that "for the sake of mankind's survival beyond the 21st century, we should seek enlightenment from the Chinese sage—Confucius."

The phenomenal economic success of Japan and the "four lesser Asian dragons" since the 1960s has astonished the world. This region is in the Oriental or East Asian cultural realm, characterised by the Confucian philosophy as its mainstream, particularly in terms of social ethics. Scholars may have different assessments of the influence of Confucianism on the development of the East Asian economy, but they differ only on the extent and magnitude of such influence rather than its existence.

During his visit to China in 1984, Japanese Prime Minister Nakasone had a discussion with the late Chinese Communist Party General Secretary Hu Yaobang in which Mr. Nakasone said that Japan had followed the footsteps of the United States and Europe in economic development, but had continued to be guided by Confucian philosophy in social ethics and moral education. Hu later commented that in the perspective of Japan's experience, Nakasone's remarks were very well founded and deserved deep pondering in China.

In recent years, China sent many students to Japan to learn business management. But the Japanese said that much of their management techniques had been learned from China. For example, the famous National Electric Appliance Business College used Chinese classics like *The Great Learning*, *The Analects of Confucius*, *Mencius* and *The Classics of Filial Piety* as textbooks of business ethics. Students were encouraged to achieve high standards of virtue, companionship and excellence.

European and American scholars commend Japan for having admirably combined modernity and tradition in building a modern economy. The Japanese have an excellent work ethic and can endure hardships. They maintain strong family ties and are polite. Thus they possess all the outstanding features of Oriental civilization.

Singapore stands out among Asia's "four lesser dragons". Its citizens receive education in ethics from adolescence, using textbooks compiled a few years ago by the authorities along lines of Confucian ideology. This approach has helped to transform Singapore into a modern civilized country. A 1991 survey by an American consultancy firm regarding risks in business environment gave highest marks to Singapore workers in terms of quality, abidance by rules, work attitude and technical proficiency.

For centuries since the advent of the industrial revolution and capitalism, Western powers have dominated the world in the realms of economics and culture. However, this began to change after the economic upsurge of East Asia. A prominent American politician commented that the 21st century would be an era of the Confucian oriented Asia-Pacific economic sphere. Although some people still hold that Confucian culture impeded East Asia's economic development and social progress, this prejudice has been disproved by facts and should be discarded.

The quintessence of traditional Chinese culture can be epitomised as the harmonious coexistence of man and nature, and the great harmony of mankind. Chinese philosophy regards mankind as the centre of all beings who can decide their own destiny and achieve eternal peace. The philosophy stresses that one has to establish one's own values and maintain a proper outlook on life and the world. This idea is also of universal significance. Taken as a whole, there are also some negative points in the traditional Chinese culture. But it would be unfair to ascribe all the dross of feudal society to Chinese traditional culture.

In a decade of reform and opening since the early 1980s, China has undergone monumental changes, and its achievements have stunned the world. As the economy surges forward in the course of transformation from a planned to a market economy, social norms and moral standards have made headway. Human relations are improving. Pressing ahead and earning one's worth by honest competition—these are becoming socially accepted values. People now accord greater importance to economics, science, knowledge and culture. On the other hand, vices have cropped up in the form of money worship, corruption, self-seeking, cheating, forgery, counterfeiting, misrepresentation, larceny and robbery. These have gravely undermined social morality and grown into a public plague. We realize that economic development and the enhancement of moral standards should go hand in hand. As we push on our reform, we will preserve and carry forward the best of our own traditional culture while drawing on the cream of foreign culture, especially that of developed countries. In this way we are convinced that we will build up a new socialist culture and ethics with Chinese characteristics.

It is with this in mind that we have compiled this book of Chinese Maxims—Golden Sayings of Chinese Thinkers over Five Thousand Years. These are selections from a wealth of Chinese philosophical works. Like flowers floating in the eternal stream of history, they retain their colour and fragrance, as well as their true beauty. They will not only be useful to one's intellectual development, but will also inspire and help one to become a better person. This book meets the needs of all those who are pressing ahead with the times, who intend to cultivate themselves their whole life long, who are busily building up their career and who wish to perfect themselves by drawing on classical texts and by learning from real life. We sincerely hope these famous maxims and golden sayings from antiquity will stir readers' minds and spur them forward. This book is also meant for foreign readers, specialists or scholars, who wish to draw on the ocean of wisdom of Chinese classics. We will feel honoured and satisfied if we achieve these lofty objectives.

Gong Dafei

February 1993

编纂说明

一、编写意图

几千年来，中华民族历代哲人贤士给我们留下了许许多多充满智慧的名言，至今仍有现实的教育意义。这些名言散见于浩若烟海的古代典籍之中，除一部分广为流传以外，还有许多鲜为人知。有鉴于此，本书精选历代先哲名言，汇编成册。意在普及与发扬中国传统文化之精华，为社会主义精神文明建设服务。

二、选取原则

作为五千年文明史的积淀，中国历代先哲名言数量浩繁，不可能选编无余。本书谨从中选取部分较有代表性者，原则如下：第一，言简易赅，便于记诵，少则几个字，多则数十字。语意过于晦涩，或牵涉到历史、人物、政治情况较具体而复杂者，则尽量少选或不选。第二，兼容并收，广采博引。从学派分野上说，既以儒家为主，也包括道、墨、法、兵、佛以及文学家、艺术家的名言；时间范围，上起先秦，下至本世纪初，但以古代为主；从书籍分类学上说，经、史、子、集俱收。第三，不以学术考辨的不同见解废言。一部分古籍被某些人定为伪作，或疑为伪作，或作者时代不明，然而其中却不乏精辟之语，也不舍弃。第四，重在继承精华。本书尽量选取那些时代局限性较小，对于现代仍有明显教育意义、应当继承发扬的精华之语，而对于那些有明显时代局限性的言论，即使曾广为流传，也不在选取之列。

三、编排顺序

本书将选取的先哲名言按内容分为以下六篇：第一，立志篇；第二，学问篇（含师道、惜时、知行等内容）；第三，修身篇；第四，处世篇；第五，智谋篇（含兵家韬略等内容）；第六，为政篇。由于中国古人言论崇尚文简义博，同一段话中常涉及多方面内容，分类时编者根据言论的重点而决定，读者不必拘泥于各篇之间的界限。在一篇中，大体按照时代先后排列，但对于时代难以确考的一部分先秦经典，如《易》、《礼记》等，则按传统作法放在前列。为了便于查阅，每一条选取的语录均加编号，其中左起第一位数为篇号，其余三位数字为总体序号。在全书最后，编有根据书名或人名查找的索引。

四、注释

尽管所选语录大都明白易懂，但对于个别较生僻的字意，仍加以简明注释。

五、英译

中国先哲名言不仅对于中国读者说来是宝贵的精神财富，而且也是人类的共同精神财富。为此，我们加以英译。翻译时，力求使译文明白易懂，而不拘泥于所选文字同其前后文的关系及其具体背景。

六、编写人员

本书由宫达非、冯禹、干春松、黄德远、张星萍、刘鹏、赵巍等同志集体讨论，选编，注释，翻译最后审定。我们的工作受到了各方面的协助和支持，在此一并致谢。

Introduction

1. **Purpose**

Many maxims framed by Chinese thinkers and other great figures in various dynasties over thousands of years have been handed down to us. Containing elements of universal truths, they are today still instructive and inspiring. They come from innumerable ancient Chinese classics. Some are still well-known, but many are now unfamiliar to most people in China. With this in mind, we have selected some golden Chinese sayings from different dynasties and are publishing them in this pocket-book, to focus and popularise the essence of the traditional culture of China and to meet the needs of the spiritual reconstruction of Chinese socialism.

2. **Principles of Selection**

China, with a civilization of over five thousand years, has such a huge number of maxims that they cannot be collected in a single volume without omission. We have therefore selected representative ones on the following principles of choice:

First, they must be succinct in expression, pithy in style and easy to remember. The shortest one consists of only a few Chinese characters and the longest no more than a few dozen characters. We have avoided maxims obscure in meaning, and ones which can only be fully understood by referring to their historic or political background.

Secondly, they must be all-embracing in attitude and from diverse sources. They should include different schools of thought. The majority selected comes from Confucianism, but pithy sayings of Taoism, Mohism, Legalism, and the School of Military Strategy are also included. Though the selection pays more attention to ancient sayings, it covers a span from pre-Qin times to the beginning of this century. All the four sections into which Chinese writings are traditionally divided—the classics, the historic books, the books of various masters, and the books of literature — have been used as sources for selection.

Thirdly, sayings have not been rejected merely because of doubts about their precise attribution. Quite a few Chinese classics have been proved — or suspected by modern specialists — not to be authentic, or wrongly dated and mistakenly attributed. As long as they are valuable maxims, we have not been reluctant to choose them, because of their spiritual value rather than their authors or dates.

Fourthly, a stress on the essence. What we have selected are golden sayings with the greatest instructive contents, least hampered by historic limitations. Any saying with evident short-comings due to historic limitations has been left out, even if it is quite popular.

3. **Arrangement**

The maxims in this volume are classified under six headings: 1. On Will; 2. On Learning (sayings on how to teach, on valuing time, and on the relationship between knowledge and action, are included in this section); 3. On Self-cultivation; 4. On Social Relations; 5. On Wisdom and Strategy; 6. On Government.

Since Chinese thinkers in ancient times appreciated that a statement should be pithy in style and rich in meaning, a single maxim may contain many interpretations and nuances. We have classified the sayings in line with the main emphasis of each maxim, but readers need not feel bound by this. In each chapter, the maxims are generally arranged in date sequence. However, maxims from classics of the pre-Qin times, such as the *Book of Changes* and the *Book of Rites*, have been put before others in accordance with traditional cataloguing. For readers' convenience, all the maxims have been given a four-digit code number. The first digit of each code number indicates the chapter to which the maxim belongs, and the other three numbers simply indicate their running sequence. An index of titles and/or authors is at the end of the book.

4. **Annotation**

Although most of the maxims are easy to understand, we have provided brief, clear annotations on some difficult words.

5. **English Translation**

The maxims selected in this book are treasures of the mind not only for Chinese but also for foreign readers. That is why we have translated the maxims into English. Our translation has tried to make the meaning of each maxim clear and comprehensible without being bogged down in its historic context.

6. **Editors and Translators**

The maxims have been selected and translated into English by Gong Dafei, Feng Yu, Gan Chunsong, Huang Deyuan, Zhang Xingping, Liu Peng and Zhao Wei. We would like to express our thanks to the many people who have made valuable suggestions and given substantial help to our work.

一、立 志 篇

Chapter 1.　On Will

1001

玩人丧德，玩物丧志。

《尚书·仲虺之诰》

[英译]

Too many fair weather friends can lose one's virtues; over-indulgence in pastimes will lose one's aspirations.

1002

身可危也，而志不可夺也。

《礼记·儒行》

[英译]

You can damage the body of a Confucian, but you cannot break his will.

1003

士不可以不弘毅。任重而道远。仁以为己任，不亦重乎？死而后已，不亦远乎？

《论语·泰伯》

[英译]

A gentleman cannot but have a grand and indomitable will for there are significant tasks for him to achieve and a long journey ahead of him. He should consider benevolence as a duty. This is a great aim and he should continue his endeavors until the end of his life.

1004

三军可夺帅也,匹夫不可夺志也。

《论语·子罕》

[英译]

It is possible to deprive an army of its commander, but you cannot deprive the people of their will.

1005

饱食终日,无所用心,难矣哉!

《论语·阳货》

[英译]

How can a man be sated with food and care for nothing else?

1006

志不强者智不达。

《墨子·修身》

[英译]

He who does not have a strong will can never achieve high intelligence.

1007

居天下之广居,立天下之正位,行天下之大道,得志与民由之,不得志独行其道,富贵不能淫,贫贱不能移,威武不能屈,此之谓大丈夫。

《孟子·滕文公下》

[英译]

The world is his home; and his position is established; the Great Tao is his way of action. If this ideal is accepted, he will pursue it with the multitudes; if not, he will go on alone. Riches and nobility cannot make him proud; poverty and humbleness cannot make him give up his aspirations; power and force cannot sway him. Such is a great man.

1008

人皆可以为尧舜。

《孟子·告子下》

[英译]

Everyone is able to become a great sage as Yao or Shun.

1009

天将降大任于是人也,必先苦其心志,劳其筋骨,饿其体肤,空乏其身,行拂乱其所为,所以动心忍性,曾益其所不能。

《孟子·告子下》

[英译]

When Heaven is about to place a great burden on a man, it always tests his resolution first, exhausts his body and makes him suffer great hardships, frustrates his efforts to recover from mental lassitude. Then Heaven toughens his nature and makes good his deficiencies.

1010

哀莫大于心死,而人死亦次之。

《庄子·田子方》

[英译]

The most tragic blow for one is the death of his mind. The death of his person is second.

1011

人无善志,虽勇必伤。

《淮南子·主术训》

[英译]

With good intentions, a man cannot cause harm even though he is powerful.

1012

燕雀安知鸿鹄之志哉!

《史记·陈涉世家》

[英译]

How can a sparrow know the will of a swan?

1013

此鸟不飞则已,一飞冲天;不鸣则已,一鸣惊人。

《史记·滑稽列传》

[英译]

This bird, though taking a rest now, will reach straight to the sky once it spreads its wings; and though silent now it will surprise people with its cries.

1014

丈夫为志，穷当益坚，老当益壮。

《后汉书·马援传》

［英译］

When in dire straits, a man should stand fast, and even more so when he is old.

1015

男儿要当死于边野，以马革裹尸还葬耳，何能卧床上在儿女手中邪？

《后汉书·马援传》

［英译］

It is better for a man to die in defence of his country and his remains brought home in a horse's hide than to stay at home and die in bed surrounded by his children.

1016

有志者事竟成也。

《后汉书·耿弇传》

［英译］

Where there is a will, there is a way.

1017

不闻大论，则志不宏；不听至言，则心不固。

《申鉴·杂言》

[英译]

Turning a deaf ear to great sayings and words of perfection one cannot have grand aspirations or a stable mind.

1018

老骥伏枥，志在千里；烈士暮年，壮心未已。

曹操《步出夏门行》

[英译]

An old horse in the stable still aspires to gallop a thousand miles. Just as a hero in the evening of his life does not give up his lofty aspirations.

1019

鞠躬尽瘁，死而后已。

诸葛亮《后出师表》

[英译]

Until death, I would spare no effort in the performance of my duty.

1020

志行万里者，不中道而辍足；图四海者，非怀细以害大。

《三国志·吴书·陆逊传》

[英译]

One who is ambitious to travel ten thousand miles will not pause half way. And one who aims at governing all within the four oceans will not be deterred by minor matters and miss the significant ones.

1021

登山,不以艰难而止;积善,不以穷否而怨。

《抱朴子·广譬》

[英译]

Climbing a mountain, one should not give up when in difficulties. Accumulating merit, one should not complain about fate.

1022

人生不能得行于胸怀,虽寿百岁,犹为夭也。

《宋书·殷琰传》

[英译]

Even if a man died at the age of hundred and had not turned his aspirations into reality, it would still be considered an early death.

1023

愿乘长风破万里浪。

《宋书·宗悫传》

[英译]

I wish to sail straight ahead with the strongest wind through the roughest sea of ten thousand miles.

1024

大丈夫宁可玉碎，不能瓦全。

《北齐书·元景安传》

[英译]

A gentleman would rather die honourably than live shamefully.

1025

丹可磨，而不可夺其色；兰可燔，而不可灭其馨；玉可碎，而不可改其白；金可销，而不可易其刚。

《刘子·大质》

[英译]

Cinnabar can be ground into dust, yet its colour remains the same; orchids can be put into fire, yet its fragrance linger; jade can be broken into pieces, yet it is still pure; metals can be smelted, yet they remain hard.

1026

老当益壮，宁移白首之心；穷且益坚，不坠青云之志。

王勃《滕王阁序》

[英译]

Age should make one stronger, and it should by no means change the mind of the white-haired. Misfortune should make one more steadfast and should not frustrate his lofty ambitions.

1027

大丈夫必有四方之志。

李白《上安州裴长史书》

[英译]

A great man must be ambitious for success in everything and every place.

1028

大凡物不得其平则鸣。……人之于言也亦然,有不得已者而后言,其歌也有思,其器也有怀,凡出乎口而为声者其皆有弗平者乎?

韩愈《送孟东野序》

[英译]

Generally speaking, things not in harmony will make a noise... The utterances of human beings are similar. They will not speak out until they have to do so. Their songs express certain ideas, and their cries present their emotions. Aren't all their statements made when they feel injustice?

1029

为天地立心，为生民立道，为去圣继绝学，为万世开太平。

张载《张子语录》

［英译］

To make a mind for Heaven and Earth, to set up the Tao for human beings, to restore the lost teachings of the past sages, and to build a peaceful world for all future generations.

1030

志不可慢，时不可失。

程颢《二程集・论五霸札子》

［英译］

Never may the will be relaxed, never may time be wasted.

1031

古之谓豪杰之士者，必有过人之节。人情有所不能忍者，匹夫见辱，拔剑而起，挺身而斗，此不足为勇也。天下有大勇者，卒然加之而不惊，无故加之而不怒。此其所挟持者甚大，而其志甚远也。

苏轼《留侯论》

［注释］

挟持：抱负。

［英译］

Those who were called heroes in ancient times must have been of extraordinary character. When they feel unbearably insulted, ordinary people will rage to thrust their swords boldly and to step forword for fighting. Such persons can not be considered brave. As for those of extraordinary courage, they will never be frightened when insults suddenly fall upon them, and they will never rage even though they face deliberate insults. The reason for this lies in the fact that their business is very significant and their aspirations are far greater.

1032

古之立大事者,不唯有超世之才,亦必有坚忍不拔之志。

苏轼《晁错论》

[英译]

Those who achieved great successes in the ancient times possessed not only extraordinary talents but also indomitable wills.

1033

生当作人杰,死亦为鬼雄。

李清照《夏日绝句》

[英译]

Should one when living be of the elite,
Dead, a heroic ghost he will become.

1034

士之所以能立天下事者，以其有志而已，然非才则无以济其志，非术则无以辅其才。

朱熹《朱子语类》

［英译］

Only a determined man will achieve worldwide success. Nevertheless, determination cannot be realised without talent and talent would be helpless without a correct method.

1035

立志要如饥渴之于饮食。才有悠悠，便是志不立。

朱熹《朱子语类》

［英译］

To establish one's will, one should be as urgent as he who desires drink and food when he is thirsty and hungry. Once there is a hint of relaxation, there is a loss of will.

1036

志小不可以语大事。

陆九渊《语录》

［英译］

One who aspires to the unimportant is not worthy of mention in the context of what is important.

1037

必有天下之大志，而后能立天下之大事。

陈亮《汉论·高帝朝》

[英译]

It is only after one has an aspiration affecting the whole world that can he achieve worldwide success.

1038

为文不能关教事，虽工无益也；笃行而不合于大义，虽高无益也；立志不存于忧世，虽仁无益也。

叶适《赠薛子长》

[英译]

However carefully composed, an article is still useless if it contains nothing instructive; the most difficult and demanding action is still useless if it does not accord with the righteousness; the most benevolent will is still useless if it cannot remove the sufferings of the world.

1039

立志须是光明正大。人多有好资质，纯粹静淡，甚近道，却甘心为卑陋之归，不肯志于道，只是不能立志。

《北溪字义·志》

[英译]

The will should be set up in a brilliant, righteous, and magnificent way. Many are well endowed with the characteristics of purity and quietness and can overcome desires. In this they are very close to Tao. Nevertheless, they are most willing to lead a base and mean life; they do not aspire to Tao. The sole reason is that they cannot establish a good will.

1040

立志要高不要卑。……立志要定不要杂,要坚不要缓。

《北溪字义·志》

[英译]

Set up a lofty will, not a base one. ... Set up a steadfast will, not a changeable one. Set up an indomitable will, not a slack one.

1041

大丈夫立志已决,若山岳之不可移也,安能随时而俯仰,触物而低昂哉?

耶律楚材《西游录》

[英译]

Once already set up, the will of a gentleman should be like a mountain, which cannot be moved. How could it vary frequently with the passage of time and shift in different environments?

1042

人须立志,志立则功就。天下古今之人,未有无志而建功。

《明太宗实录》

[英译]

Man ought to cultivate a good will, and thus achieve his aim. No one, throughout the whole world and whole history, could achieve success without a good will.

1043

志不立，天下无可成之事。虽百工技艺，未有不本于志者。

王阳明《训俗遗规》

[英译]

Without setting up a will, nothing in the world can be accomplished. Even craftsmanship is based on the will.

1044

已立志为君子，自当从事于学。凡学之不勤，必其志之尚未笃也。

王阳明《教条示龙场诸生》

[英译]

Once he has made up his mind to be a gentleman, one should necessarily be engaged in learning. If he is not diligent, it is because his will is not strong enough.

1045

为学当先立志，修身当先知耻。

傅山《霜红龛集》

[英译]

To be resolute is the prerequisite of learning, and knowing what shame is the prerequisite of self-cultivation.

1046

学者志不立，一经患难，愈见消沮，所以先要立志。

《宋元学案》

[英译]

A student who has not yet achieved firmness of mind must become frustrated as soon as he encounters difficulties. Therefore the foremost thing for him to do is to be resolute.

1047

大凡为学，先须立志，志大而大，志小而小。有有志而不遂者矣，未有无志而成者也。

张履祥《初学备忘》

[英译]

Generally speaking, one who intends to learn must be determined first and foremost. With great determination, one's achievement in learning will be great; with lack of will, his achievement will be small. There are some who show determination but still fail to succeed in learning. Without the will however there is no prospect of success.

1048

天下无难事，只怕有心人。

王骥德《题红记》

［英译］

Nothing is impossible for those who have a strong will.

二、为 学 篇

Chapter 2. On Learning

2049

好问则裕，自用则小。

《尚书·仲虺之诰》

［英译］

Through constant consultations with others, one will have ample knowledge. Too self-assertive will make one narrow-minded.

2050

玉不琢，不成器；人不学，不知义。

《礼记·学记》

［英译］

Without carving, a piece of jade cannot be turned into an ornament or be used as a sacrifice. Without learning, a man cannot know what righteousness is.

2051

学然后知不足，教然后知困。

《礼记·学记》

［英译］

One can hardly know the limit of his knowledge until he begins to learn, and when he teaches he will learn there are still many unsolved problems.

2052

善问者，如攻坚木，先其易者，后其节目。及其久也，相说以解。不善问者反此。

《礼记·学记》

[注释]

节目:指关键部位。

[英译]

He who is always asking questions will act in a way similar to cutting hard wood. He will begin with the easy parts and then work on the main branches. Eventually the whole thing will be understood through the mutual explanation of the learned parts. He who does not ask questions will do just the contrary.

2053

教学相长。

《礼记·学记》

[英译]

Those who teach and those who learn may improve each other.

2054

善歌者使人继其声,善教者使人继其志。

《礼记·学记》

[英译]

A good singer makes his audience ask for more of his songs. A good teacher makes his students carry on his ideals.

2055

记问之学，不足以为人师。

《礼记·学记》

[英译]

He whose knowledge is obtained only by rote learning and consultation is not qualified to be a teacher.

2056

凡学之道，严师为难。师严，然后道尊。道尊，然后民知敬学。

《礼记·学记》

[英译]

About learning, the most difficult thing is to find strict teachers. Only when the teachers are strict, can the students appreciate the Tao. Only when the Tao is appreciated, can people respect learning.

2057

君子之教喻也，道而弗牵，强而弗抑，开而弗达。

《礼记·学记》

[注释]

道：通“导”。

[英译]

A gentleman's way of teaching is to guide the students instead of pushing them. He will encourage them to learn rather than supress them, and he will open the way to truth instead of telling them the answers to all their questions.

2058

善待问者如撞钟，叩之以小则小鸣，叩之以大则大鸣。

《礼记·学记》

［英译］

A teacher who is good at answering students' inquiries is like a bell being struck. Being slightly struck, it will ring in a low voice; being heavily struck, it will ring loud.

2059

君子有三患：未之闻，患弗得闻也；既闻之，患弗得学也；既学之，患弗能行也。

《礼记·杂记》

［英译］

A gentleman has three worries: Not yet being informed of a good thing, he worries until he knows. When he knows, he begins to worry he has not yet learned it. When he learns it, he begins to worry he has not yet put it into practice.

2060

好学近乎知，力行近乎仁，知耻近乎勇。知斯三者，则知所以修身；知所以修身，则知所以治人；知所以治人，则知所以治天下国家矣。

《礼记·中庸》

[英译]

Fond of learning, one gets close to wisdom; to practice hard, one gets close to benevolence; knowing what shame is, one gets close to courage. If one knows all these three aspects, he will know how to cultivate himself. Knowing how to cultivate himself, he will know how to manage people. Knowing how to manage people, he will know how to rule the world.

2061

博学之,审问之,慎思之,明辨之,笃行之。

《礼记·中庸》

[英译]

Learn avidly! Question what you have learned repeatedly! Think over them carefully! Analyse them intelligently! Put what you believe into practice diligently!

2062

有弗学,学之弗能,弗措也。有弗问,问之弗知,弗措也。有弗思,思之弗得,弗措也。有弗辨,辨之弗明,弗措也。有弗行,行之弗笃,弗措也。

《礼记·中庸》

[注释]

措:废弃。

[英译]

It doesn't matter if you have not yet started to learn something. When you have started, however, you must not stop until you really know it. It doesn't matter if you have not yet asked questions, but when you begin, you must not stop until you are satisfied. It doesn't matter if you have not yet started to think carefully, but when you do, stop only when you have reached a conclusion. It doesn't matter if you have not yet started to discern something, but when you have, you must not stop until you are clear. It doesn't matter if you have not yet started to practise something, but when you do, you must diligently put it into practice.

2063

人一能之,己百之;人十能之,己千之。果能此道矣,虽愚必明,虽柔必强。

《礼记·中庸》

[英译]

While others are able to know something by learning it once, you should learn it a hundred times; while others are able to know it by learning it score of times, you should learn it a thousand times. If you can really do things in such a way, you would be intelligent even though you had been foolish, and you would be strong even though you had been weak in the beginning.

2064

言以足志,文以足言。不言,谁知其志?言之无文,行而不远。

《左传·襄公二十五年》

[英译]

Language is a supplement to a will, and literature is a supplement to speech. Whithout language, who can know your will? Without literature language cannot be disseminated.

2065

人求多闻善败,以监戒也。

《国语·楚语下》

[注释]

监:通"鉴"。

[英译]

People should be shown the importance of previous examples of success and failure in order to use them as lessons.

2066

君子食无求饱,居无求安,敏于事而慎于言,就有道而正焉,可谓好学者也已。

《论语·学而》

[英译]

A gentleman does not engage in seeking food to satisfy his stomach and comfortable house to live in. Instead, he is diligent in his duties and careful of his words. And he follows those who have the knowledge of Tao and corrects himself according to it. In so doing, he can be called a man who is fond of learning.

2067

吾十有五而志于学,三十而立,四十而不惑,五十而知天命,六十而耳顺,七十而从心所欲,不逾矩。

《论语·为政》

[英译]

At the age of fifteen, I made up my mind to learn; at thirty, I was already well established; at forty I began to be immune from confusion; since the age of fifty, I have known the Decrees of Heaven; since the age of sixty, I have felt no surprise at any opinion; and in my seventies, I have been able to do whatever I intend to without breaching the rules.

2068

温故而知新,可以为师矣。

《论语·为政》

[英译]

If one can have new inspirations by reviewing what he learned before, he is qualified to be a teacher.

2069

学而不思则罔,思而不学则殆。

《论语·为政》

[注释]

罔:迷惘。

殆:危险。

[英译]

Confused is one who learns without pondering. Endangered is one who ponders without learning.

2070

发愤忘食，乐以忘忧，不知老之将至。

《论语·述而》

[英译]

So diligent and occupied am I in learning as to forget meals, and so great a rejoicing have I attained in it as to forget all worries and sorrows. In such a mood, I even forget I am getting old.

2071

三人行必有我师焉。择其善者而从之，其不善者而改之。

《论语·述而》

[英译]

Among three people I meet on the way, there will be at least one from whom I can learn something. I may follow his goodness or correct my own mistakes by learning from him.

2072

吾尝终日不食，终夜不寝，以思。无益，不如学也。

《论语·卫灵公》

[英译]

Once I tried to contemplate all day and all night without eating and sleeping to no effect. It is not as good as learning.

2073

有教无类。

《论语·卫灵公》

[英译]

Education should be for all, irrespective of their social status.

2074

好仁不好学,其蔽也愚。好知不好学,其蔽也荡。好信不好学,其蔽也贼。好直不好学,其蔽也绞。好勇不好学,其蔽也乱。

《论语·阳货》

[注释]

荡:奸佞。

贼:伤害。

绞:急躁。

[英译]

It is a foolish man who likes benevolence but dislikes learning. If one respects wisdom but dislikes learning, he will be crafty. If one likes sincerity but dislikes learning, he will be easily harmed. If one likes straightforwardness but dislikes learning, he will be rough. If one likes courage but dislikes learning, he will be a hooligan.

2075

仕而优则学，学而优则仕。

《论语·子张》

［英译］

An outstanding offical should be educated to improve his knowledge while an outstanding scholar should be charged with official duties to practise what he has learned.

2076

善弓者师弓不师羿，善舟者师舟不师奡，善心者师心不师圣。

《关尹子·五鉴》

［注释］

羿：古代善射者。

奡：古代善驾舟者。

［英译］

He who is good at shooting arrows learns through his own bow instead of Yi (a master archer). He who is good at rowing learns through rowing his own boat instead of Ao (one of the best oarsmen). He who is good at thinking learns through his own mind instead of instruction from the sages.

2077

虽有天下易生之物也，一日暴之，十日寒之，未有能生者也。

《孟子·告子上》

[英译]

Even the strongest plant could hardly survive if it were exposed to sunshine one day but to the cold for ten days.

2078

今夫弈之为数，小数也。不专心致志，则不得也。弈秋，通国之善弈者也。使弈秋诲二人弈，其一人专心致志，惟弈秋之为听；一人虽听之，一心以为有鸿鹄将至，思援弓缴而射之。虽与之俱学，弗若之矣。

《孟子·告子上》

[注释]

弈：古代围棋。

缴：系着丝线的箭。

[英译]

Though playing chess is but an inferior skill, one cannot learn it well if one is not attentive. Suppose Yi Qiu, the best chess master of the country, is teaching two fellows to play chess. While one of them learns attentively and concentrates on listening to the master, the other, although he also listens to the master, thinks that a swan may be flying by and he should shoot it down with an arrow. Although the latter learns chess together with the former, his skill cannot match that of the former.

2079

心之官则思。思则得之，不思则不得也。

《孟子·告子上》

[英译]

The role of heart is thinking. It is by thinking that one can attain knowledge. And one cannot attain knowledge without thinking.

2080

尽信书则不如无书。

《孟子·尽心下》

[英译]

We would rather be short of books than believe all that they say.

2081

孔子登东山而小鲁,登泰山而小天下,故观于海者难为水,游于圣人之门者难为言。

《孟子·尽心下》

[英译]

Climbing Mt. Dong, Confucius felt the State of Lu was small. Climbing Mt. Tai, he felt the whole under Heaven was small. Therefore, after seeing the magnificence of the ocean, the rivers can hardly be still proud of immense quantity of water. After being educated by a sage, who can give a speech?

2082

路漫漫其修远兮，吾将上下而求索。

屈原《离骚》

[英译]

Long as the way is, I will keep on searching above and below.

2083

学不可以已。青，取之于蓝而青于蓝；冰，水为之而寒于水。木直中绳，輮以为轮，其曲中规，虽有槁暴，不复挺者，輮使之然也。故木受绳则直，金就砺则利，君子博学而日参省乎己，则知明而行无过矣。

《荀子·劝学》

[注释]

蓝：可以加工青色颜料的植物。
輮：通"揉"，使弯曲。
槁：干燥。
暴：日晒。
参：通"叁"，即三。

[英译]

There is never an end to learning and self-improvement. The dye extracted from the indigo plant is bluer than indigo, and ice is colder than water. A piece of wood as straight as a tight string, if bent to form a wheel, may become so round that it can stand the examination by a compass. Later, even if it be heated and dried, it will not turn straight again. Similarly, a piece of wood can be made straight by the help of a tightened string, and a piece of metal can be sharpened by honing on a stone. A gentleman who has been learning widely and examines his actions three times a day, can have an intelligent mind and make no mistakes.

2084

吾尝终日而思矣，不如须臾之所学也；吾尝跂而望矣，不如登高之博见也。

《荀子·劝学》

［注释］

跂：踮起脚尖。

［英译］

Once I contemplated a whole day but what I gained was less than what I would get by a moment's learning. Once I stood on tiptoe in order to look farther, yet what came in my sight was inferior to what I would get by looking on a higher elevation.

2085

不积跬步，无以至千里；不积小流，无以成江海。骐骥一跃，不能十步；驽马十驾，功在不舍。锲而舍之，朽木不折；锲而不舍，金石可镂。

《荀子·劝学》

［注释］

跬步：半步。

骐骥：良马。

驽马：能力低下的马。

［英译］

Without the accumulation of small steps, a one-thousand-mile journey cannot be finished; without the accumulation of the streamlets, there would be no confluence of a great river or the sea. The fastest horse cannot reach ten steps at one leap, yet an ordinary horse can gallop a great distance by continuous trotting. Halting halfway, one could not even carve a piece of decayed wood into two parts; If, on the contrary, he never stops till the completion of carving, he could even carve those as hard as metal or stone.

2086

不闻不若闻之,闻之不若见之,见之不若知之,知之不若行之。学至于行之而止矣。行之,明也,明之为圣人。圣人也者,本仁义,当是非,齐言行,不失毫厘,无他道焉,已乎行之矣。故闻之而不见虽博必谬;见之而不知,虽识必妄;知之而不行,虽敦必困。

《荀子·儒效》

［英译］

Not to hear a thing is no better than to hear it; to hear it is no better than to see it; to see it is no better than to understand it; to understand it is no better than to practise it. The learning of this ends by practising it. Practice is the proof of enlightenment and the enlightened are sages. A sage accords with benevolence and righteousness, correctly tells right from wrong, and his words matches his deeds without error. There is no other way than practice to become a sage. Therefore, hearing without seeing, one may be outrageous though broadly learned; seeing without understanding, one may be false though rich in knowledge; understanding without practising, one may be frustrated though he may have profound vision.

2087

君子之学,非为通也,为穷而不困,忧而意不衰也,知祸福终始而心不惑也。

《荀子·宥坐》

[英译]

For a gentleman, the aims of learning are not the rapid advances in his career, but that he feels no difficulty in adversity, he feels no frustration when worried, and his mind is not confused because he knows there is a beginning and end of fortune and misfortune.

2088

不知礼义,生于不学。

《吕氏春秋·劝学》

[英译]

The ignorance of the ceremonies and righteousness comes out of the shortage of learning.

2089

古之圣王未有不尊师者也,尊师则不论其贵贱贫富矣。

《吕氏春秋·劝学》

[英译]

There were no ancient sage-kings who did not respect teachers. Irrespective of a teacher's social status and properties, they were revered.

2090

不知则问,不能则学。

《吕氏春秋·谨听》

[英译]

Not knowing something, consult those who know; unable to do something, learn from those who are able.

2091

不能则学,不知则问,虽知必让,然后为知。

《韩诗外传》

[英译]

The learned is one who learns whatever he is unable, consults with others about what he does not know, and remains modest after he has got knowledge.

2092

智如泉涌,行可以为表仪者,人师也。

《韩诗外传》

[英译]

Endless is his wisdom, and his conduct a good model to follow. Such a man is qualified to be teacher.

2093

圣人以身体力行。

《淮南子·氾论训》

[英译]

A sage practice what he preaches.

2094

圣人不贵尺之璧,而重寸之阴,时难得而易失也。

《淮南子·原道训》

[注释]

璧:环状玉器。

[英译]

A sage does not value a large jade but cherishes a moment of time for time is difficult to keep and very easy to lose.

2095

知无务,不若愚而好学。

《淮南子·修务训》

[英译]

It is better to be dull though fond of learning than to be clever but idle.

2096

功者难成而易败，时者难得而易失。时乎，时乎，不再来。

《史记·淮阴侯列传》

［英译］

Merits are hard to achieve but easy to fail in the trials to achieve them. Time is hard to grasp but easy to lose. Alas! Time! It will never come again!

2097

书犹药也，善读之可以医愚。

《说苑·建本》

［英译］

Books are like medicine. Reading them in a correct way may cure people's foolishness.

2098

讯问者，智之本；思虑者，智之道也。

《说苑·建本》

［英译］

Consultation is the basis of wisdom and contemplation is the way to wisdom.

2099

人材虽高，不务学问，不能致用。

《说苑·说丛》

[英译]

Even though endowed with high talent, one would be useless without learning and consultation.

2100

君子不羞学,不羞问。

《说苑·说丛》

[英译]

A gentleman never feels shameful to learn from and to consult with others.

2101

人而不学,虽无忧,如禽何?

《法言·学行》

[英译]

In case a man refuses to learn, though he might have no worries now, is there any difference between him and an animal?

2102

圣人之于天下,耻一物之不知。

《法言·君子》

[英译]

A sage would still feel shameful even though there was only one thing left beyond his knowledge.

2103

常玉不琢，不成文章；君子不学，不成其德。

《汉书・董仲舒传》

[注释]

文章：指光彩。

[英译]

A piece of jade could not have brilliant colors without polishing; a gentleman could not perfect his virtues without learning.

2104

百闻不如一见。

《汉书・赵充国传》

[英译]

Hearing is no better than seeing.

2105

修学好古，实事求是。

《汉书・河间献王传》

[英译]

One should pursue learning diligently, be fond of the ancient classics, and seek truth from facts.

2106

不学自知，不问自晓，古今行事，未之有也。

王充《论衡・实知》

[英译]

In both past and the present, there is no such man who attains knowledge without learning and understands without consultation.

2107

不学不成，不问不知。

王充《论衡·实知》

[英译]

No learning, no achievement; no consultation, no knowledge.

2108

知古不知今，谓之陆沉。知今不知古，谓之盲瞽。

王充《论衡·谢短》

[注释]

陆沉：泥古不化，腐儒。

[英译]

He who knows the past but not the present is called a pedant. He who knows the present but not the past is blind.

2109

人有知学，则有力矣。

王充《论衡·效力》

[英译]

Powerful is one who has knowledge.

2110

世俗之性,好奇怪之语,说虚妄之文。何则?实事不能快意,而华虚惊耳动心也。是故才能之士,好谈论者,增益其事,为美盛之语;用笔墨者,造生空文,为虚妄之传。听者以为真然,说而不舍;览者以为实事,信而不绝。

王充《论衡·对作》

[注释]

说:通"悦",喜爱。

[英译]

Ordinary people admire eccentric words and enjoy unreal and fantastic remarks. Why? Because reality and facts can rarely please their minds whereas beautiful but unreal words astonish and attract them. For this reason, talented scholars who are fond of talking always exaggerate true facts and speak in flowery language; writers compose unreal articles and create false and fantastic stories. People take what they say to be true and are pleased. Reading about unreality, people accept them as true facts and believe in them so they continue without end.

2111

虚妄之语不黜,则华文不见息;华文放流,则实事不见用。

王充《论衡·对作》

[注释]

华文:华而不实之文。

[英译]

If unreal and fantastic words are not abandoned, beautiful but false writings will not cease. If beautiful but false writings spread widely, people will be unable to act upon the truth.

2112

人生在勤,不索何获?

《后汉书·张衡传》

[英译]

The meaning of life is to strive. Without pursuit, what can one achieve?

2113

导人必因其性,治水必因其势。

《中论·贵言》

[英译]

Guiding the people, one must follow their nature; taming rivers, one must accord with their natural tendency.

2114

学者如登山焉,动而益高。

《中论·治学》

[英译]

The pursuit of learning is like climbing. With each step the climber moves higher.

2115

少壮不努力,老大徒伤悲。

《乐府诗集·长歌行》

[英译]

Idleness when young, regrets before long.

2116

读书百遍,其义自见。

《三国志·魏志》

[英译]

When a book is read a hundred times, its meanings will naturally become clear.

2117

人之学,如渴而饮河海,大饮则大盈,小饮则小盈;大观则大见,小观则小见。

《意林·物理论》

[英译]

For a student, to learn is similar to that of a thirsty man drinking from the river and the sea. If he drinks much, he gains much; if he drinks too little, he gains little. If he sees learning with a greater perspective, he will have a greater insight; if he sees it from a smaller perspective, he will have less insight.

2118

学而不思，则疑阂实繁；讲而不精，则长惑丧功。

葛洪《抱朴子·博喻》

[注释]

阂：阻碍。

实：是。

繁：多。

[英译]

Learing without deep thought, one will have many unsolved problems. Wide discussions without precise analysis, one will cause confusion and nothing will be achieved.

2119

不学而求知，犹愿鱼而无网焉，心虽勤而无获矣。

葛洪《抱朴子·勖学》

[英译]

To want knowledge but unwilling to learn is like fishing without a net. He may be anxious, yet he gains nothing.

2120

不饱食以终日，不弃功于寸阴。

葛洪《抱朴子·勖学》

[英译]

Do not spend days on just eating or waste your time.

2121

人好学，虽死犹存；不学者，虽存，谓之行尸走肉耳。

《拾遗记》

［英译］

With love of learning, man's spirit lives on after the decay of his body. Unwilling to learn, even though alive, he is but a walking corpse.

2122

大禹圣者，乃惜寸阴；至于众人，当惜分阴。

《晋书・陶侃传》

［英译］

A sage, the Great Yu still valued every minute of time. Thus, people should value every second of time.

2123

臣闻行百里者半九十，言其末路之难也。

《宋书・颜延之传》

［英译］

It is said "Ninety miles is only half of a hundred-mile journey", thereby suggesting the final stage of a course is the most difficult.

2124

万物有好丑，各以姿状论；喻人则不尔，不学与学论。

《金楼子・杂编上》

[英译]

A myriad things are divided into the beautiful and the ugly. As for mankind, the standard is whether they are learned.

2125

读书万余卷，一事不知，以为深耻。

《南史·陶弘景传》

[英译]

Even if one had read ten thousand volumes and there was only one thing left out of his knowledge, he should still feel ashamed.

2126

观天下书未遍，不得妄下雌黄。

《颜氏家训·勉学》

[英译]

One is not qualified to give opinions until he has read books from all over the world.

2127

夫学者犹种树也，春玩其华，秋登其实；讲论文章，春华也；修身利行，秋实也。

《颜氏家训·勉学》

[英译]

Learning is like planting trees which enables one to enjoy their blossom in the spring and to harvest their fruits in the autumn. The discussion and comment on books and articles resemble the blossom in the spring, whereas the self-cultivation and application of the knowledge to society resemble the fruits in the autumn.

2128

积财千万,不如薄技在身。

《颜氏家训·勉学》

[英译]

One would rather learn a simple skill than accumulate enormous wealth.

2129

君子下学而无常师,小人耻学而羞不能。

《群书治要·体论》

[英译]

A great man should learn from everybody, even those who are inferior to him. He should not learn from one teacher alone. An inadequate man feels ashamed to learn from others and reluctant to acknowledge his ignorance.

2130

欲穷千里目,更上一层楼。

王之涣《登鹳鹊楼》

[英译]

To get a broader view, climb to another floor of the tower.

2131

黑发不知勤学早，白首方悔读书迟。

颜真卿《劝学》

[英译]

To spend one's youth at leisure at the expense of reading will be too late for regrets in the evening of one's life.

2132

读书破万卷，下笔如有神。

杜甫《杜工部集》

[英译]

He owns a gifted pen, who reads tremendously.

2133

古之学者必有师。师者，所以传道、授业、解惑也。人非生而知之者，孰能无惑？惑而不从师，其为惑也，终不解矣。

韩愈《师说》

[英译]

In ancient times, one had to find a teacher when he began to learn. A teacher is one by whom the courses are taught and the Tao is handed down to the students. Under this teacher's guidance, the perplexities of the students are removed. Man is not endowed with knowledge when he is born. Who then can avoid them? Where man is confused but refuses to consult with a teacher, his perplexities will never be removed.

2134

生乎吾前，其闻道也，固先乎吾，吾从而师之；生乎吾后，其闻道也，亦先乎吾，吾从而师之。吾师道也，夫庸知其年之先后生于吾乎？是故无贵无贱，无长无少，道之所存，师之所存也。

韩愈《师说》

［英译］

He who is older than me and has learned about Tao before I do, will be considered a teacher for me to follow. Even if he is younger and has also learned about Tao before me, he will also be considered a teacher to follow. Since that is my desire, then, is there any necessity to know whether a teacher is older or younger than me? Wherever Tao exists a teacher will be found, irrespective of his age and social status.

2135

是故弟子不必不如师，师不必贤于弟子，闻道有先后，术业有专攻，如是而已。

韩愈《师说》

［英译］

A student is not inferior to his teacher, and a teacher is not superior to his student. The difference between a teacher and student is, the former knows Tao earlier and they each have their own expertise.

2136

业精于勤，荒于嬉；行成于思，毁于随。

韩愈《进学解》

［英译］

Learning is perfected through diligence and ruined by idleness. Actions are accomplished through prudence and destroyed by ignorance.

2137

学如牛毛，成如麟角。

《蒋子万机论》

［英译］

Countless are those who make a beginning in learning, yet scarcely any of them can accomplish it.

2138

君子好学不厌，自强不息，推之使远，廓之使大，耸之使高，研之使深，发于心，形于身，裕于家，施于国，格于上下，被于四表。

《司马文正公传家集》

［注释］

廓：扩展。

耸：推崇。

格：至。

［英译］

A gentleman is eager and tireless in learning and makes unremitting efforts to improve himself. He always tries to extend the knowledge he has learned further, to expand it greater, to exalt it higher, and to explore it deeper. The knowledge that comes out of his mind will be formed in his behaviour, fulfilled in his family, applied to his country, presented to above and below, and endowed in all directions.

2139

学者贵于行之，而不贵于知之。

司马光《答孔文仲司马户书》

[**英译**]

About learning, practice is more valuable than mere understanding.

2140

人多是耻于问人。假使今日问于人，明白胜于人，有何不可？

张载《张子全书·学大原》

[**英译**]

Most people feel ashamed to consult with others. If today's consultation brings tomorrow's superiority to those with whom they consult, what reason is there to be ashamed?

2141

人若志趣不远，心不在焉，虽学无成。

《经学理窟·义理》

[英译]

If one has no high aspirations or cannot concentrate, one will achieve nothing even though a beginning in learning has been made.

2142

学贵心悟,守旧无功。

《经学理窟·义理》

[英译]

The most valuable thing in learning is to understand with one's own mind, and it is useless to persist with the old dogma.

2143

懈意一生,便是自暴自弃。

《二程集·遗书》

[英译]

To be relaxed all through life is to give oneself up as hopeless.

2144

人之于学,避其所难而姑为其易者,斯自弃也矣。夫学者必志于大道,以圣人自期,而犹有不至者焉。

《河南程氏粹言·论学篇》

[英译]

If a man tries to elude difficulties in learning but works only on the easy things, he has given up. As a learner, he must aspire after the Great Tao with ambition to become a sage. Even so, he may make no achievement in learning.

2145

君子之学必日新,日新者日进也。不日新者必日退,未有不进而不退者。

《河南程氏粹言·论学篇》

[英译]

The learning of a gentleman is characterised by daily renewal and daily renewal brings about daily progress. If one cannot renew his knowledge daily, he will certainly lose ground daily. It is rare for one to neither progress or regress.

2146

知之必好之,好之必求之,求之必得之。

《河南程氏粹言·论学篇》

[英译]

Like it if you want to know something. Seek it if you like it. Get it if you are searching for it.

2147

言愈多,于道未必明,故言以简为贵。

《河南程氏粹言·论学篇》

[英译]

Flowery words may not be necessary proof of one's clear understanding of Tao. Therefore, the succinct expression is more appreciated.

2148

力学而得之,必充广而行之。

《河南程氏粹言·论学篇》

[英译]

If you have learned something through hard study, extend it and put it into practice.

2149

莫等闲,白了少年头,空悲切。

岳飞《满江红》

[英译]

Do not idle when young, for when old in years regret comes along.

2150

学欲博,不欲杂;守欲约,不欲陋。

《胡子知言·仲尼》

[英译]

What one learns should be abundant but not miscellaneous; it should be simple and not narrow.

2151

古人学问无遗力，少壮功夫老始成。

陆游《冬夜读书示子聿》

［英译］

Ancient people spent all their efforts in learning because they understood that the efforts they made when young would not be successful until they were older.

2152

纸上得来终觉浅，绝知此事要躬行。

陆游《冬夜读书示子聿》

［英译］

Superficial is the knowledge gained through mere reading. The only way to gain real knowledge is in practise.

2153

人之病只知他人之说可疑，而不知己说之可疑。试以诘难他人者以自诘难，庶几自见得失。

朱熹《朱子语类》

［注释］

庶几：接近，差不多。

［英译］

It is a common mistake that a man only suspects the ideas of others and never suspects his own ideas. If he can question himself in the same way as he questions others, he will be halfway towards finding his strong and weak points.

2154

学之之博，未若知之之要；知之之要，未若行之之实。

朱熹《朱子语类》

［英译］

To learn broadly is not so good as to grasp the fundamental, and to grasp the fundamental is not so good as to put it into practice.

2155

读书无疑者，须教有疑；有疑者，却要无疑，到这里方是长进。

朱熹《朱子语类》

［英译］

If a student cannot raise any questions in his reading, the teacher should teach him. If a student raises many questions, however, the teacher should help him. Progress is made through such shifts.

2156

君子之道，不以其所已能者为足，而尝以其未能者为歉，一日课一日之功，月异而岁不同，孜孜矻矻，死而后已。

《陈亮集》

［注释］

孜孜矻矻：勤奋不懈。

［英译］

A gentleman should not be satisfied with what he can but always look for what he cannot. Each day he should complete his set tasks with the contents varying with each passing month and year. He should continue learning without stop untill the end of his life.

2157

工贵其久，业贵其专。

《陈亮集》

［英译］

Continuous efforts promise good work, and concentration benefits a profession.

2158

学不必博，要之有用；仕不必达，要之无愧。

《鹤林玉露·学仕》

［英译］

For learning, the necessary requirement is not the attainment of a wide range of knowledge but the usefulness of such knowledge. For a career, the necessary requirement is not rapid promotion but a clear conscience.

2159

绳锯木断，水滴石穿。

《鹤林玉露·学仕》

[英译]

Not giving up halfway, a string may saw a piece of wood, and drops of water may penetrate a piece of stone.

2160

至博而约于精,深思而敏于行。

方孝孺《书签》

[英译]

Learn widely but do not neglect the essential; be profound in thinking but diligent in practice.

2161

不患其无才,患其无学;不患其不任,患其不忠;不患其无功,患其无志。

王廷相《慎言》

[英译]

Do not worry if you have no talent, but worry if you have no knowledge. It is more important to be loyal than to have an official post. Do not worry if you cannot succeed, but worry if you have no aspirations.

2162

广识未必皆当,而思之自得者真;泛讲未必吻合,而习之纯熟者妙。

王廷相《慎言》

[英译]

Not all what one learns is correct. Only knowledge gained through deep consideration are real. What one discusses widely are not necessarily identical with facts, only those which have been repeatedly practised are the genuine ones.

2163

读万卷书，行万里路。

董其昌《画旨》

[英译]

Read as many books as you can. Travel as long as the way may be.

2164

读书不能身体力行，便是不能读书。

《陈确集·文集》

[英译]

If one reads many books but cannot practise what he has learned thereby, he should be considered one who cannot read.

2165

学问之道无他，惟时时知过改过。无不知，无不改，以几于无可改，非圣而何？

《陈确集·瞽言一》

[英译]

Learning means nothing but to find out one's faults and correct them immediately. Once all the faults have been corrected and there are few mistakes to correct, what will such a man be if not a sage?

2166

学固未可以言尽也。

《陈确集·瞽言一》

[英译]

Learning is indeed an endless course.

2167

为学须是一鼓作气,间断便非学,所谓"再而衰"也。

《宋元学案》

[英译]

Learning should be pursued with continuous efforts. Any interruption in the process means that it has been given up, just as the proverb says, "To start again indicates decline".

2168

君子之为学也,非利己也。有明道淑人之心,有拨乱反正之事,知天下之势之何以流极而至于此,则思起而有以救之。

顾炎武《亭林余集》

[注释]

淑:使善。

[英译]

When a man studies, his aim is not just benefiting himself. Instead, he has the understanding of Tao and can improve the people's well-being, and participate in overcoming the political disorders and helping a perverse society back on the right road. As soon as he knows why the situation is worsening to such an extreme, he will come to secure the world.

2169

才以用而日生，思以引而不竭。

王夫之《周易外传》

[英译]

Talent is daily refreshed in active use, and thinking is not exhausted by positive function.

2170

有不知则有知，无不知则无知。

王夫之《张子正蒙注》

[英译]

A man will have knowledge when he realises that there are things still outside of his knowledge. If a man states that there is nothing he doesn't know, then he is an ignorant man.

2171

学而必习，习又必行。

颜元《习斋言行录》

[英译]

After learning, one must review. After reviewing, one must practise.

2172

世事洞明皆学问,人情练达好文章。

曹雪芹《红楼梦》第五回

[英译]

Everything to do with day to day living constitutes learning, and a deeper understanding about the emotions of ordinary people constitutes true knowledge.

2173

学问之道,其得之不难者,失不必易。唯艰难以得之者,斯能敬业以守之。

魏源《默觚·学篇》

[英译]

Learning easily mastered must also be easy to forget. Only what is gained with painstaking effort can be held fast.

2174

及之而后知,履之而后艰,乌有不行而能知者乎?

魏源《默觚·学篇》

[英译]

Only personal experience can man know; only after he practises, can he know the difficulties. Is there any knowledge gained without practice?

2175

古之成大业者,多自克勤小物而来。百尺之楼,基于平地;千丈之帛,一尺一寸所积也。

曾国藩《曾文正公全集·杂著》

[英译]

Those who have achieved success since ancient times began their tasks through diligent work on the smaller issues, for they knew that the building of a tall edifice has to begin with its foundations, and a piece of silk of thousand meters has to be made by accumulating the weaving of every thread.

2176

能知而不能行者,非真知也,真知则无不能行矣。

谭嗣同《仁学》

[英译]

If one knows theory but cannot put it into practice, then it may not be real knowledge. On the contrary, if it is real knowledge, then it can be put into practice.

三、修身篇

Chapter 3. On Self-cultivation

3177

天行健,君子以自强不息。

《易·象·乾》

[英译]

As Heaven keeps active and vigorous, a gentleman makes unremitting efforts to improve himself.

3178

善不积,不足以成名。恶不积,不足以灭身。小人以小善为无益而弗为也,以小恶为无伤而弗去也,故恶积而不可掩,罪大而不可解。

《易·系辞下》

[英译]

Without accumulation, one's merits are not enough to bring fame. Without accumulation, one's demerits are not enough to bring self-destruction. Believing a small merit not useful, inferior men do not achieve it. Believing a small demerit to be harmless, they do not overcome it. As a result, their demerits will accumulate till they become notorious, and their sins will become so great that they cannot be blotted out.

3179

白圭之玷,尚可磨也;斯言之玷,不可为也。

《诗经·大雅·柳》

[注释]

圭:玉器。

[英译]

Stain upon white jade may still be removed by polishing, but stain upon a speech can by no means be removed.

3180

见利不亏其义,……见死不更其守。

《礼记·儒行》

[英译]

Do not seek profits at the cost of righteousness. ... Nor change your conduct under the threat of death.

3181

诚其意者,毋自欺也。

《礼记·大学》

[英译]

By "making one's mind sincere", it is meant that one should not cheat oneself.

3182

修身在正其意。

《礼记·大学》

[英译]

The key to self-cultivation is to make one's mind just.

3183

善不可失,恶不可长。

《左传·隐公六年》

［英译］

Do not lose the chance of doing good, nor encourage the evil.

3184

俭,德之共也;侈,恶之大也。

《左传·庄公二十四年》

［英译］

Frugality is the common requirement of all sorts of virtues whereas extravagance is the worst of all sorts of evils.

3185

窃人之财,犹谓之盗,况贪天之功以为己力乎?

《左传·僖公二十四年》

［英译］

Those who steal others' belongings are called thieves, let alone those who arrogate to themselves the merits of Heaven.

3186

死而不义,非勇也。

《左传·文公二年》

［英译］

Not even death can bring the fame of bravery to one who is not in accordance with righteousness.

3187

人谁无过，过而能改，善莫大焉。

《左传·宣公二年》

［英译］

Mistakes cannot be avoided. If one can correct mistakes after committing them, then one will win the greatest merit.

3188

怙其隽才，而不以茂德，兹益罪也。

《左传·宣公十五年》

［注释］

怙：凭恃。
隽：通“俊”。

［英译］

Blame is to be attributed to one who relies on great talent and not on great virtue.

3189

人之所以立，信、知、勇也。

《左传·成公十七年》

［英译］

It is with sincerity, wisdom, and courage that one establishes a firm standing.

3190

惟善,故能举其类。

《左传·襄公三年》

[注释]

类:指善同于己之人。

[英译]

Only he who is himself good can promote those whose virtues are similar.

3191

君子之行,思其终也,思其复也。《书》曰:"慎始而敬终,终以不困。"

《左传·襄公二十五年》

[英译]

When a gentleman begins an action, he always considers how to end and reverse it. As the *Book of Documents* says: "If one keeps cautious in the beginning and reverent at the end, he will be free from troubles".

3192

上德若谷,大白若辱,广德若不足。

《老子》41 章

[英译]

Superb virtue is as open as a valley; great purity looks like something stained; even one possessing many such qualities seems deficient.

3193

吾日三省吾身:为人谋而不忠乎？与朋友交而不信乎？传不习乎？

《论语·学而》

[英译]

I examine myself three times daily: Have I done something unfaithful to others? Have I done something insincere to my friends? Have I reviewed what I learned?

3194

今之学者,是谓能养。至于犬马,皆能有养。不敬,何以别乎？

《论语·为政》

[英译]

In accordance with present scholars, [filial piety] implies nothing but that one should provide adequately for the support of his parents. However, even dogs and horses can provide for the supports of their parents. If one does not pay reverence to his parents, is there any difference between him and an animal?

3195

朝闻道,夕死可也。

《论语·里仁》

[英译]

I would never regret dying in the evening if only I could learn about Tao in that morning.

3196

君子喻于义,小人喻于利。

《论语·里仁》

[英译]

A great man has a good knowledge of righteousness whereas a small man has that of profit-making.

3197

富与贵,是人之所欲也。不以其道得之,不处也。贫与贱,是人之所恶也。不以其道得之,不去也。

《论语·里仁》

[英译]

Everyone desires wealth and higher rank. Nevertheless, one should not accept them if his aim is not achieved in a right way. Everyone dislikes poverty and lower rank. Nevertheless, one should not try to get rid of them if his aim is not achieved in a right way.

3198

古者言之不出，耻躬之不逮也。

《论语·里仁》

[英译]

In olden times, people did not talk much for fear that their deeds could not meet their words.

3199

君子欲讷于言而敏于行。

《论语·里仁》

[英译]

A gentleman would rather be quick in action than talk a lot.

3200

知者乐水，仁者乐山。知者动，仁者静。知者乐，仁者寿。

《论语·雍也》

[英译]

The wise are delighted by water, the benevolent by mountains; the wise appreciate movement, the benevolent quietude; the wise lead a happy life, the benevolent are long-lived.

3201

饭疏食，饮水，曲肱而枕之，乐亦在其中矣。不义而富且贵，于我如浮云。

《论语·雍也》

[注释]

疏:粗。

肱:手臂。

[英译]

I would still feel happy even if I had to eat coarse food, drink nothing but water, and take my arms as a pillow when asleep. Wealth and higher rank, if gained without righteousness, mean no more than a flying cloud to me.

3202

仁远乎哉?我欲仁,斯仁至矣。

《论语·雍也》

[英译]

Is benevolence far from us on earth? Only if I wanted it, would it come to my side.

3203

君子坦荡荡,小人长戚戚。

《论语·雍也》

[英译]

A superior man is broad-minded whereas small-minded man is always resentful.

3204

岁寒,然后知松柏之后凋也。

《论语·子罕》

[英译]

Only in freezing winter, can we realise that pines and cypresses are cold-resistant.

3205

志士仁人,无求生以害仁,有杀身以成仁。

《论语·卫灵公》

[英译]

It is never the case that a man of lofty ideals and benevolence would do things illicit to preserve his life, and there are times when he would sacrifice his life for the completion of benevolence.

3206

人能弘道,非道弘人。

《论语·卫灵公》

[英译]

It is man who can make Tao great, and not Tao that makes man great.

3207

过而不改,是谓过矣。

《论语·卫灵公》

［英译］

A real mistake is committed when one refuses to correct his mistakes.

3208

巧言乱德，小不忍则乱大谋。

《论语·卫灵公》

［英译］

Cunning speech destroys virtues, and lack of tolerance for petty annoyances destroys significant plans.

3209

君子有三戒：少之时，血气未定，戒之在色。及其壮也，血气方刚，戒之在斗。及其老也，血气既衰，戒之在得。

《论语·季氏》

［注释］

得：贪得。

［英译］

There are three admonitions for a gentleman: When young and unable to control the sap of youth, the admonition for him is not to indulge in lust; when grown up to the prime of life and at his most robust, his admonition is not to get into fights; when aged and declining in energy, his admonition is not to be too greedy.

3210

见善如不及，见不善如探汤。

《论语·季氏》

[注释]

汤：开水。

[英译]

At the sight of something good, one should immediately learn it as if he would otherwise miss the chance forever. At the sight of something bad, one should immediately draw back as if he had put his hands into boiling water.

3211

道听途说，德之弃也。

《论语·阳货》

[英译]

One who is fond of hearsay gives up his virtues.

3212

君子之过也，如日月之食焉，人皆见之。更也，人皆仰之。

《论语·子张》

[英译]

Like the eclipses of the sun and the moon, the mistakes of a superior man are in clear sight of the multitude. When he corrects them, however, the people will hold him in higher reverence.

3213

君子惠而不费，劳而无怨，欲而不贪，泰而不骄，威而不猛。

《论语·尧曰》

[英译]

A superior man is generous but not wasteful; he is diligent without complaint; he has desires but is not greedy; he is great but not arrogant thereby; he is awesome but not fierce.

3214

非其道，则一箪食不可受于人。如其道，则舜受尧之天下，不以为泰。

《孟子·滕文公下》

[注释]

泰：过分。

[英译]

If against Tao, one should not accept even a basketful of food from others. When he was in accordance with Tao, Shun accepted everything under Heaven from Yao without considering it excessive.

3215

夫人必自辱，然后人辱之。家必自毁，而后人毁之。国必自伐，而后人伐之。

《孟子·离娄上》

[英译]

Only when one invites insult will others insult him. Only when a family invites destruction will others destroy it. Only when a state invites invasion will others invade it.

3216

自暴者,不可与有言也。自弃者,不可与有为也。言非礼义,谓自暴也。吾身不能居仁义,谓之自弃也。

《孟子·离娄上》

[英译]

It is impossible to talk seriously with those who are self-defeating; it is impossible to persuade those who are self-abandoned into action. By self-defeating, we mean those whose speech is ever against the ceremonies and righteousness; by self-abandoned, we mean those who declare that they cannot lead a life of benevolence and righteousness.

3217

道在迩而求诸远,事在易而求诸难。

《孟子·离娄上》

[英译]

Tao lies at hand yet many tend to seek it afar; things are easy yet they try to resolve them in the most difficult way.

3218

人有不为也,而后可以有为。

《孟子·离娄上》

[英译]

Only when one does not do something will he be capable of doing [significant] things.

3219

君子有终身之忧,无一朝之患也。

《孟子·离娄上》

[英译]

While a superior man has perpetual worries, he has no unexpected and sudden vexations.

3220

鱼,我所欲也。熊掌,亦我所欲也。二者不可得兼,舍鱼而取熊掌者也。生,亦我所欲也;义,亦我所欲也。二者不可得兼,舍生而取义。

《孟子·离娄上》

[英译]

Fish is what I desire, and bear's paw is also what I desire. In case I cannot have both, I would rather take the bear's paw than fish. Just as life is what I cherish, and righteousness is also what I cherish. In case I cannot have both, I would rather take righteousness than life.

3221

仰不愧于天，俯不怍于人。

《孟子·尽心上》

［注释］

怍：惭愧。

［英译］

Do nothing shameful to Heaven above，nor things shameful to people below.

3222

至人无己，神人无功，圣人无名。

《庄子·逍遥游》

［英译］

A perfect man does not hold himself in regard；a godlike man does not expect any merit；and a sage pays no attention to renown.

3223

真者，精诚之至也。不精不诚，不能动人。

《庄子·渔父》

［英译］

Verity means perfect purity and honesty. Without purity and honesty，one cannot move others.

3224

自知者不怨人，知命者不怨天；怨人者穷，怨天者无志。失之己，反之人，岂不迂乎哉！

《荀子·荣辱》

[英译]

He who knows himself well never complains against others. He who knows his fate well never complains against Heaven. He who complains against others will find no way out. He who complains against Heaven will lose his will. The failure is caused by himself yet he shifts blames to others. Is not such a man foolish?

3225

君子崇人之德，扬人之美，非谄谀也；正义直指，举人之过，非毁疵也；言己之美，拟于舜禹，参于天地，非夸诞也；与时屈伸，柔从若蒲苇，非慑怯也；刚强猛毅，靡所不信，非骄暴也。以义变应，知当曲直故也。

《荀子·不苟》

[注释]

蒲苇：水生植物。

慑：恐惧。

信：伸张。

[英译]

It is not flattering when a superior man exalts the merits of others and praise them highly. It is not defamation when he makes direct criticism of them and discloses their mistakes. It is not boasting when he announces his own merits, compares them to those of Shun and Yu, and considers them even identical with those of Heaven and Earth. It is not fear when he shifts his attitude and looks sometimes as soft as pliable as reeds. It is not despotism or violence when he acts in such a mighty and straightforward way that all obstacles are swept away. The reason why he does so is that he varies and responds to things in accordance with righteousness and that he knows well about the propriety.

3226

岁不寒，无以知松柏，事不难，无以知君子。

《荀子·大略》

[英译]

The nature of pines and cypresses cannot be found until the freezing winter comes; the character of a superior man cannot be seen until great difficulties come upon him.

3227

君子耻不修，不耻见污；耻不信，不耻不见信；耻不能，不耻不见用。

《荀子·非十二子》

[英译]

A superior man feels ashamed that he fails in cultivation, not that he is slandered; that he is untruthful, not that he is distrusted by others; that he lacks capability not that he gets no official appointment.

3228

良农不为水旱不耕，良贾不为折阅不市，士君子不为贫穷怠乎道。

《荀子·修身》

［英译］

A good farmer does not give up ploughing the land because of flood or drought. A good merchant does not stop doing business because of unexpected losses. A real gentleman does not relax his pursuit after Tao because of poverty and hardship.

3229

道虽迩，不修不至；事虽小，不为不成。

《荀子·修身》

［英译］

Although Tao is close at hand, one cannot get it without self-cultivation. Although a thing is by no means difficult, one cannot accomplish it without making efforts.

3230

君子易知而难狎，易惧而难胁，畏患而不避义死，欲利而不为所非，交亲而不比，言辩而不辞，荡荡乎，其有以殊于世也。

《荀子·不苟》

［英译］

A superior man is easy to know but hard to know deeply. He is timid but hard to threaten. Though in fear of perils, he is willing to sacrifice his life for righteousness. He refuses, though desiring benefits, any profit-making action that may put him to shame. He makes close friends but never forms a clique with them. He is eloquent but never speaks empty words. So great is him that shows a sharp contrast to the ordinary people.

3231

君子宽而不慢,廉而不刿,辩而不争,察而不激,直立而不胜,坚强而不暴,柔从而不流,恭敬谨慎而容,夫是之谓至文。

《荀子·不苟》

[注释]

刿:刺伤。

容:从容。

[英译]

A superior man is lenient but not easy-going; fair but not severe; eloquent but not quarrelsome; clear but not critical; straightforward but not arrogant; unyielding but not fierce; agreeable but not servile; respectful, cautious while calm. Such a gentleman is called highly civilised.

3232

义之所在,身虽死,不憾悔。

《战国策·秦策》

[英译]

I will not regret even death as long as I stand firm with righteousness.

3233

宁为鸡口,无为牛后。

《战国策·韩策》

[英译]

Rather would I be the head of a cock than the tail of an ox.

3234

功莫美于去恶而为善,罪莫大于去善而为恶。

《新书·修政语上》

[英译]

No achievement is better than removing evil and doing good; no sin is greater than giving up good and doing evil.

3235

放情者危,节欲者安。

《盐铁论》

[英译]

Undisciplined passion causes perils and the control of desires results in safety.

3236

卑而言高,能言而不能行者,君子之耻矣。

《盐铁论》

[英译]

It is considered shameful for a gentleman to deliver lofty remarks while behaving in an ignoble way, failing to match his words with deeds.

3237

士不以利移,不为患改。

《说苑·说丛》

[英译]

A superior man never changes his mind for profits nor wavers in the face of perils.

3238

君子之言寡而实,小人之言多而虚。

《说苑·说丛》

[英译]

A superior man talks little but it is the truth; whereas an inferior man talks much, but it is false.

3239

诚无诟,思无辱。

《说苑·敬慎》

[英译]

Honesty prevents defilement and thinking prevents disgrace.

3240

修身以为弓，矫思以为矢，立义以为的，奠而后发，发必中矣。

《法言·修身》

[注释]

奠：定。

[英译]

Take self-cultivation as a bow，rectification of thought as an arrow，and the establishment of righteousness as a target. Shoot after quieting your mind. When this is done，the arrow will certainly hit the target.

3241

重言，重行，重貌，重好。言重则有法，行重则有德，貌重则有威，好重则有观。……言轻则招忧，行轻则招辜，貌轻则招辱，好轻则招淫。

《法言·修身》

[注释]

辜：辜累。

[英译]

Be cautious in speech. Be cautious in action. Be cautious in appearance. Be cautious in appreciation. Cautious speech is certainly in accordance with laws. Cautious action is certainly virtuous. Cautious appearance inspires awe. Cautious appreciation is of good mannered. ... On the contrary，careless words lead to worries. Careless actions lead to troubles. Careless appearance leads to shame.

Careless appreciation leads to lust.

3242

处逸乐而欲不放，居贫穷而志不倦。

《论衡·自纪》

［英译］

Be not wanton when in leisure and pleasure. Neither be frustrated when in poverty and hardship.

3243

止谤莫如修身。

《中论·道虚》

［英译］

The best way not to slander another is to devote onself to self-cultivation.

3244

才敏过人未足贵也，博辩过人未足贵也，勇决过人未足贵也；君子之所贵者，遇善惧其不及，改过恐其有余。

《中论·道虚》

［英译］

It is not of value that one is more talented and quicker in understanding than others, that one is more abundant in knowledge and eloquent in speech than others, and that one is more fearless and resolute than others. What matters to a gentleman is the fear that he cannot catch up with those who are good and that he cannot correct his mistakes completely.

3245

君子必贵其言，贵其言则尊其身，尊其身则重其道，重其道所以立其效。

《中论·贵言》

[英译]

A superior man surely cares much for his language so he will be held in high esteem. When he is held in high esteem, the Tao he follows will be highly appreciated. With such approbation, the language of a superior man is received with respect.

3246

良将不怯死以苟免，烈士不毁节以求生。

《三国志·魏志·庞德传》

[英译]

A good general never escapes from battles through fear of death. A hero never saves his life at the cost of his conduct.

3247

勿以恶小而为之，勿以善小而不为。

《三国志·蜀志·先主传》

[英译]

Do not do evil things though they may be insignificant. Do not give up good things though they may be minor matters.

3248

百炼而南金不亏其真，危困而烈士不失其正。

《抱朴子·博喻》

[注释]

南金：纯金，一说为一种玉石。

[英译]

A piece of finest gold always keeps its purity even though it is melted a hundred times. A hero never loses justice even though subject to peril and hardship.

3249

浮假者无功。

《文心雕龙·丽辞》

[英译]

One who is superficial and hypocritical achieves nothing.

3250

生以救时，死以明道。

《中说·周公》

[英译]

Try to secure society from dangers when alive. Die a heroic death to illustrate Tao.

3251

不为苟得以偷安，不为苟免而无耻。

《群书治要·体论》

［英译］

Do not seek ignoble safety, nor to preserve life with disgrace.

3252

言非法度不出于口，行非公道不萌于心。

杨炯《杜袁州墓志铭》

［英译］

Speak nothing against laws and regulations, and think nothing against justice.

3253

松柏本孤直，难为桃李颜。

李白《松柏本孤直》

［英译］

Straightforward, pines and cypresses stand alone, unlike peaches and plums which seek appreciation through the colors of their blossom.

3254

谁言寸草心，报得三春晖。

孟郊《游子吟》

［英译］

Never enough is the gratitude of grass for the grace of the spring sun.

3255

圣人非不好利也，利在于利万人；非不好富也，富在于富天下。

白居易《第林·不夺人利》

［英译］

The sages did not dislike benefits, but they tried to benefit the people. They did not dislike riches, but they tried to enrich the whole world.

3256

周乎志者，穷踬不能变其操；周乎艺者，居抑不能贬其名。

柳宗元《柳河东集》

［注释］

周：圆满，圆极。

踬：跌倒，挫折。

居抑：处在艰难环境中。

［英译］

With one who has perfect will, hardship and failure cannot change his conduct. With one who has perfect capacity, temporary depression cannot lessen his fame.

3257

春蚕到死丝方尽,蜡炬成灰泪始干。

李商隐《无题》

[英译]

Till the end of life a silk worm keeps spinning silk. Till burning itself out a candle goes on lighting us.

3258

所守者道义,所行者忠信,所惜者名节。

欧阳修《朋党论》

[英译]

Persist in Tao and righteousness. Act on loyalty and sincerity. Cherish fame and reputation.

3259

予独爱莲之出淤泥而不染,濯清涟而不妖,中通外直,不蔓不枝,可远观而不可亵玩焉。予谓:菊,花之隐逸者也;牡丹,花之富贵者也;莲,花之君子者也。

周敦颐《爱莲说》

[英译]

The reason why I love lotus alone is that it grows in sludge but keeps clean, bathes in green water but is not a coquette, is smooth inside and straight outside, has neither frivolous stems nor worthless branches, can be appreciated only from afar but does not tolerate indecent approaches. Therefore, I make the statement that the chrysanthemum is "the recluse" among flowers, peony "the rich and of high rank", and lotus "the noble and virtuous" of the flowers.

3260

圣人之道,仁义中正而已矣。守之贵,行之利,廓之配天地。岂不易简,岂为难知?不守不行不廓耳。

周敦颐《通书·道》

[英译]

The Tao of the sages contains no more than benevolence, righteousness, moderation, and justice. Persisting in it, one becomes noble; acting upon it, one benefits from it; extending it, one is able to compare oneself to Heaven and Earth. Is not Tao easy and simple? Is it difficult to understand? The only reason why people fail to comprehend is that they do not persist in it, act upon it, and extend it.

3261

实胜,善也;名胜,耻也。故君子进德修业,孳孳不息,务实胜也。德业有未著,则恐恐然畏人知,远耻也。小人则伪而已。故君子日休,小人日忧。

周敦颐《通书·务实》

[英译]

When reality surpasses reputation, it is good. When reputation transgresses reality, it is a shame. Therefore, a gentleman will make diligent and tireless efforts in the promotion of his virtue and the perfection of his profession in order that his reality may surpass his reputation. When he has not yet achieved obvious success in virtue and in his profession, he will be greatly afraid of renown that he can keep away from shame. An inferior man, on the contrary, will seek a false reputation. Thus, the superior will be at ease and the inferior will suffer worries daily.

3262

淡则欲心平,和则躁心释。

周敦颐《通书·乐上》

[英译]

Nonchalance calms down the desires and peace expels impetuosity.

3263

君子以道充为贵,身安为富,故常泰无不足,而铢视轩冕,尘视金玉。

周敦颐《通书·富贵》

[注释]

铢:古代重量单位,为二十四分之一两,此处形容极轻。

轩冕:指高官厚禄。

[英译]

A gentleman will consider it noble that his mind is filled with Tao, and he will consider it riches that his body is at ease. Therefore, he always feels peaceful instead of insufficient. He looks down upon high official posts and gold and jade.

3264

人情苦厌其所有,羡其所不可得。未得则羡,已得则厌,厌而求新,则为恶无不至矣。

司马光《司马文正公传家集》

[英译]

It is a common characteristic to be sick and tired of things already obtained and to feel envy at things one is unable to obtain. Thus, when one has not yet obtained something, he feels envy about it. Once he achieves it, however, he will be tired of it and seek something new. Thereby every kind of evil may be committed.

3265

贫贱忧戚,庸玉女于成也。

《正蒙·乾称》

[注释]

戚:悲伤。

女:通"汝"。

玉女于成:使你成功。

[英译]

Poverty, humbleness, depression and woe all greatly help a man to achieve great success.

3266

日省其身,有则改之,无则加勉。

朱熹《四书集注》

[英译]

One should examine himself daily. When he finds faults, he should correct them. When he finds none, he should urge himself to do better.

3267

生无以救国难,死犹为厉鬼以击贼。

文天祥《指南录后序》

[英译]

Since I have failed to secure my country from calamity during my life time, I wish I could become a fierce ghost to attack the foe after my death.

3268

人生自古谁无死,留取丹心照汗青。

文天祥《过零丁洋》

[英译]

Since death is unavoidable to everyone throughout history, what one should strive for is a loyal heart, gloriously recorded in the historic books.

3269

防微杜渐而禁于未然。

《元史·张桢传》

[英译]

Evils should be prevented before they are fully developed.

3270

千锤万凿出深山，烈火焚烧若等闲。粉身碎骨浑不怕，要留清白在人间。

于谦《石灰吟》

[英译]

I came as a piece of limestone painfully dug out of wild mountains. The rage of flames is immaterial to me. Since I have no fear of being reduced to powder, the only hope I have is to keep my purity and cleanliness in the world.

3271

宁学圣人而不至，不从一善而成名。

王阳明《寄福安诸同志》

[英译]

I would rather be seen to fail in the pursuit of sagehood, than to win a reputation in pursuit of what is mediocre.

3272

学者于贫贱富贵不动其心，死生祸福不变其守，则天下之事无不可为矣。

王廷相《慎言》

[英译]

Nothing is beyond the reach of a scholar who cannot be disturbed by poverty or riches, humbleness or nobility. Death and life, fortune and misfortune, can bring about no effect in his conduct.

3273

气忌盛,心忌满,才忌露。

吕坤《呻吟语·人品》

[英译]

No impetuosity. No arrogance. No showing off.

3274

知过之谓智,改过之谓勇,无过之谓仁。

《陈确集·瞽言一》

[英译]

Wisdom means to find out one's own mistakes. Courage means the correction of those mistakes. Benevolence means to make no mistakes.

3275

成德每在困穷,败身多因得志。

魏象枢《寒松堂集》

[英译]

Virtue is often achieved by those who have encountered poverty and hardship. Disgrace and ruin often befall those who have satisfied their ambitions.

3276

天地生财，只有此数，由俭入奢易，由奢返俭难。人当时时猛省。

张伯行《困学录集粹》

[英译]

The wealth supplied by Heaven and Earth is finite, and people are willing to shift from frugality to extravagance, but unwilling to shift from extravagance to frugality. One should always remember this.

3277

惟敬可以胜怠，惟勤可以补拙，惟俭可以养廉。

张伯行《困学录语粹》

[英译]

It is reverence that can overcome laziness. It is diligence that can make up the shortage of wisdom. And it is frugality that can secure one from corruption.

3278

智也者，言乎其不蔽也；仁也者，言乎其不私也；勇也者，言乎其自强也；非不蔽不私加以自强，不可诱于智仁勇。

戴震《孟子字义疏证》

[注释]

诱：教导。

[英译]

Wisdom denotes the absence of obsession; benevolence denotes unselfishness; courage denotes self-strengthening. Instruction in wisdom, benevolence and courage may not be given to people except those who are not obsessive, unselfish, and self-strengthening.

3279

蜗牛升壁,涎不干不止;贪人求利,身不死不休。

申居郧《西岩赘语》

[英译]

A snail climbing a wall will not stop until the attempt consumes all its strength; similarly, a greedy man will keep on seeking wealth till the end of his life.

四、处 世 篇

Chapter 4. On Human Relations

4280

居上位而不骄，在下位而不忧。

《周易·文言》

[英译]

No complacence when ranked high; no anxiety when low.

4281

二人同心，其利断金。

《周易·系辞上》

[英译]

When two men are one in heart, they will get such a strength that metal can be easily cut.

4282

君子上交不谄，下交不渎。

《周易·系辞下》

[英译]

A gentleman neither fawns on those who are superior to him, nor slights those who are inferior.

4283

兄弟阋于墙，外御其务。

《诗经·小雅·棠棣》

[注释]

阋：争吵。

务:借为"侮"。

[英译]

Brothers, though quarreling at home, should fight together against the insult from outside.

4284

君子之道,辟如远行必自迩,辟如登高必自卑。

《礼记·中庸》

[注释]

辟:通"譬"。

[英译]

For a gentleman, the realisation of Tao is like a long journey which must start in a near place; it is like climbing a high mountain which must begin from somewhere low.

4285

圣人与众人同欲。

《左传·成公六年》

[英译]

The desire of a sage is the same as that of the multitude.

4286

多行无礼,必自及也。

《左传·襄公四年》

[英译]

He who frequently breaks the rules of ceremonies will surely bring about harm to himself.

4287

信者,言之瑞也,善之主也。

《左传·襄公九年》

[英译]

Sincerity is the treasure of speech and the centre of good conduct.

4288

临患不忘国,忠也。思难不越官,信也。图国忘死,贞也。谋主三者,义也。

《左传·昭公元年》

[英译]

To worry about one's country instead of oneself in the face of peril means loyalty; to try to resolve the most difficult problems but never to overstep one's authority means sincerity; to risk one's life for his country means justice; and to consider the three things above-mentioned as the fundamental principles of action means righteousness.

4289

无礼而好陵上,怙富而卑其上,弗能久矣。

《左传·昭公元年》

［注释］

陵：僭越。

怙：凭靠。

［英译］

He cannot last long who tends to overstep his authority and to use his wealth to slight his superiors.

4290

求逞于人，不可。与人同欲，尽济。

《左传·昭公四年》

［英译］

It is unacceptable for a person to build his joy on others' pains. If, on the contrary, he shares desires with others, he will obtain all that he desires.

4291

君子之言，信而有征，故怨远于其身。小人之言，僭而无征，故怨咎及之。

《左传·昭公八年》

［注释］

征：证明。

僭：假，不可信。

［英译］

The words of a superior man are of trust based on evidence; hence he avoids complaints. On the contrary, the words of an inferior man are of falsehood without evidence, hence he is troubled with complaints.

4292

大德灭小怨,道也。

《左传·定公五年》

[英译]

In accordance with Tao, the grudge against someone should be forgiven in consideration of his great goodness.

4293

私仇不及公,好不废过,恶不去善,义之经也。

《左传·哀公五年》

[英译]

Never do harm to the public interest because of a personal grudge. Never forgive mistakes because of personal favoritism. Never deny the goodness of those whom you dislike. These are the fundamental principles of righteousness.

4294

私欲弘侈,则德义鲜少;德义不行,则迩者远离而远者距违。

《国语·楚语》

[英译]

Extravagance in personal desires results in the lack of morality and righteousness. When a person does not behave himself in accordance with morality and righteousness, those who used to be close will leave him and those who are afar will ever keep him at a distance.

4295

唯仁者可好也,可恶也,可高也,可下也。好之不逼,恶之不怨,高之不骄,下之不惧。

《国语·楚语》

[英译]

No one but those of benevolence can keep a correct attitude towards likes and dislikes and high or low rank. When they like something, they never seek it by force. When they dislike something, they are never resentful. When they rank high, they are never arrogant. When they rank low, they never feel uneasy.

4296

轻诺者必寡信,多易者必多难。

《老子》63 章

[英译]

He who promises casually can hardly keep his words; he who always takes things easy will necessarily be troubled with many difficulties.

4297

君子周而不比，小人比而不周。

《论语·为政》

[注释]

周：亲近和谐。

比：结党营私。

[英译]

Superior men keep harmonious relations with each other but they never form cliques. On the contrary, inferior men tend to form cliques but fail to keep harmonious relations with each other.

4298

人而无信，不知其可也。大车无輗，小车无軏，其何以行之哉？

《论语·为政》

[注释]

輗：车杠前端与车衡衔接处穿孔中的关键。

軏：同輗，但用于小车。

[英译]

I do not know what use a man can be put to, whose words are untruthful. How can a wagon be made to go if it has no yoke or a carriage, or if it has no harness?

4299

君子敬而无失，与人恭而有礼，四海之内，皆兄弟也。

《论语·颜渊》

[英译]

If a gentleman always maintains reverence without ignorance, behaves with courtesy to others, and observes the rules of ritual, then all within the Four Oceans are his brothers.

4300

言必信,行必果。

《论语·子路》

[英译]

One must stand by one's words and must not stop one's action until success is achieved.

4301

君子和而不同,小人同而不和。

《论语·子路》

[英译]

Superior men appreciate harmony instead of sameness whereas inferior men appreciate sameness instead of harmony.

4302

群居终日,言不及义,好行小慧,难矣哉!

《论语·卫灵公》

[英译]

How intolerable are those who tend to spend a whole day together without ever once mentioning things righteous, but are fond of performing petty acts of cunning!

4303

君子义以为质，礼以行之，孙以出之，信以成之。

《论语·卫灵公》

[注释]

孙：通"逊"，谦虚。

[英译]

A gentleman takes righteousness as his character, the rites as a guide for his actions, honesty as the way to set out his plan, and sincerity as the means by which his plan is realised.

4304

君子病无能焉，不病人之不己知也。

《论语·卫灵公》

[英译]

A gentleman is distressed by his own lack of capacity. He is never distressed at the failure of others to recognise his merits.

4305

君子矜而不争，群而不党。

《论语·卫灵公》

[注释]

矜：坚强。

[英译]

A gentleman is unyielding but not quarrelsome; he is agreeable but not cliquey.

4306

己所不欲,勿施于人。

《论语·卫灵公》

[英译]

Never do to others what you would not like them to do to you.

4307

当仁不让于师。

《论语·卫灵公》

[英译]

When it comes to benevolence, one need not avoid competing with one's teacher.

4308

益者三友,损者三友。友直,友谅,友多闻,益矣。友便辟,友善柔,友便佞,损矣。

《论语·季氏》

[注释]

谅:诚信。
便辟:善于逢迎谄媚。
善柔:以颜色诱惑人。

便佞：以言辞取媚于人。

［英译］

There are three sorts of friends that are helpful, and three sorts that are harmful. Friendship with the upright, with the trustworthy, and with the learned is helpful. Friendship with the obsequious, with the outwardly kind but inwardly wicked, and with those of cunning words is harmful.

4309

与善人居，如入芝兰之室，久而不闻其香，即与之化矣。与不善人居，如入鲍鱼之肆，久而不闻其臭，亦与之化矣。

《孔子家语·六本》

［注释］

肆：商店。

［英译］

Like one who, after staying long in a greenhouse of orchids, can no longer smell the fragrance of the orchids, one who stays with good people will be transformed into the same as them. Like one who, after staying long in a store of salted fish, can no longer smell the offensive odour, one who stays with evil people will also be transformed into the same as them.

4310

人之患在好为人师。

《孟子·离娄上》

[英译]

A common trouble with people is that they are too eager to assume the role of teacher.

4311

君子之交淡如水,小人之交甘若醴;君子淡以亲,小人甘以绝。

《庄子·山木》

[注释]

醴:甜酒。

[英译]

Though light, the relationship between superior men is of the kind that lasts long. Though sweet, that between inferior men is easier to break.

4312

好面誉人者,亦好背而毁之。

《庄子·盗跖》

[英译]

He who is good at fawning on you in your presence will also be good at creating slander on you in your absence.

4313

为善,使人不能得从,此独善也。为巧,使人不能得从，此独巧也，未尽善、巧之理。为善与众行之，为巧与众能之，此善之善者，巧之巧者也。

《尹文子·大道上》

[英译]

If one does something good but fails to enable others to do the same, it is called personal goodness. If one does something ingenious but fails to enable others to do the same, it is personal ingenuity. Thereby, the principle of real goodness and ingenuity has not yet been fully understood. If one does good oneself and simultaneously makes others practise the same; if one does something ingenious and at the same time makes others do likewise, it will be the best among things good and the most ingenious among various kinds of ingenuity.

4314

处浊世而类荣兮，非余心之所乐。与其无义而有名兮，宁穷处而守高。

《楚辞·九辩》

[英译]

It would give me no pleasure to receive seeming splendor in such a chaotic world, and I would rather lead a poor life while persisting in lofty aspirations than get renown at the cost of righteousness.

4315

非我而当者，吾师也；是我而当者，吾友也；谄谀我者,吾贼也。

《荀子·修身》

[英译]

He who correctly criticises me is my teacher; he who correctly praises me is my friend; he who flatters me is my foe.

4316

与人善言,暖如布帛;伤人以言,深于矛戟。

《荀子·荣辱》

[英译]

Friendly words given to others are as warm as clothes whereas sharp words hurting others bring about much more pain than swords do.

4317

高上尊贵不以骄人,聪明圣智不以穷人,齐给速通不争先人,刚毅勇敢不以伤人。不知则问,不能则学,虽能必让,然后为德。

《荀子·非十二子》

[英译]

Although in high rank, he is not arrogant; although wise and intelligent, he does not make others embarrassed; although much quicker than others to learn, he does not try to parade his advance; although unyielding and brave, he does not thereby hurt others. He is not reluctant to consult with others when he does not know something; he is not reluctant to learn from others when he is not capable of doing something; he is still modest after he has been capable of doing that thing. Only when a man behaves himself in such a way, can he be considered a man of virtue.

4318

欲胜人者，必先自胜；欲论人者，必先自论；欲知人者，必先自知。

《吕氏春秋·先己》

［英译］

To surpass others, a person has to surpass himself first; to criticise others, he has to criticise himself first; to make comments upon others, he has to make comments on himself first.

4319

士为知己者死。

《战国策·赵策》

［英译］

A gentleman would even risk his life for those who really understand him.

4320

人之有德于我也，不可忘也；吾有德于人也，不可不忘也。

《战国策·魏策》

［英译］

A person must not forget the favours others did for him, but he must forget the favours he did for others.

4321

厚者不毁人以自益也,仁者不危人以要名。

《战国策·燕策》

[英译]

A man of kindness and honesty never gains advantages by doing harm to others. A man of benevolence never gets a reputation by endangering others.

4322

仁不轻绝,智不轻怨。

《战国策·燕策》

[注释]

绝:与人断交。

[英译]

A man of benevolence never breaks off relations with others recklessly. A man of wisdom never make reckless complaints against others.

4323

吾妻之美我者,私我也;妾之美我者,畏我也;客之美我者,欲有求于我也。

《战国策·齐策》

[英译]

It is because my wife is partial to me that she praises me; it is because my concubine is afraid of me that she praises me; it is because my guest wants something from me that he praises me.

4324

正其行而不苟合于世。

《新语·辨惑》

[英译]

Persist in righteous conduct and do not accommodate it to illicit customs.

4325

经瓜田不纳履,过李下不整冠。

《列女传·齐威虞姬》

[英译]

Do not tie your shoelaces in a melon field, nòr adjust your hat under a plum tree [lest you be suspected of stealing].

4326

人必其自爱也,然后人爱诸;人必其自敬也,然后人敬诸。

《法言·君子》

[英译]

It is only after one cherishes one's own conduct that it can be appreciated by others; it is only after one has self-respect that one can be respected by others.

4327

水至清则无鱼,人至察则无徒。

《汉书·东方朔传》

[注释]

察:苛求。

[英译]

No fish can survive if the water is too clean. For the same reason, no company can bear one whose requirements are too critical.

4328

欲人勿闻,莫若勿言;欲人勿知,莫若勿为。

《汉书·枚乘传》

[英译]

If you do not want to be heard, you'd better keep silent; if you do not want your actions to be seen, you'd better not start.

4329

誉人不增其美,毁人不益其恶。

《论衡·艺增》

[英译]

Neither overstate a person's merits when praising him, nor overstate his demerits when criticising him.

4330

高论而相欺，不若忠论而诚实。

《潜夫论·实质》

[英译]

To deliver exaggerated and lofty remarks in a hypocritical way is not better than to speak honestly in realistic language.

4331

峣峣者易缺，皦皦者易污。阳春之曲，和者必寡。盛名之下，其实难副。

《后汉书·黄琼传》

[注释]

峣：高貌。

皦：清白。

[英译]

Things that are too high fall down easily; things that are too white stain easily; songs that are too pretentious have few listeners; reputations that are too high often fall short of reality.

4332

贫贱之交不可忘。

《后汉书·宋弘传》

[英译]

When a person becomes rich and ranks high, he should by no means forget the old friends he made when he was still poor and humble.

4333

志合者不以山海为远，道乖者不以咫尺为近。故有跋涉而游集，亦或密迩而不接。

《抱朴子·博喻》

[英译]

If two men are one in heart, mountains and oceans cannot keep them apart. If two men do not share common ideals, there will be a great distance between them though they stand side by side. That is why some people travel across mountains and waters to meet, and others never make contact with each other though they stay together.

4334

不虚美，不隐恶，不雷同以偶俗。

《抱朴子·明本》

[英译]

Do not sing false praises, nor conceal mistakes, nor give up initiatives in order to accommodate yourself to convention.

4335

人或毁己，则退而求之于身；若己有可毁之行，则彼言当矣；若己无可毁之行，则彼言妄矣；当则无怨于彼，妄则无害于身。

《金楼子·戒子》

[英译]

When you are criticised, you should examine yourself. If you have indeed done something wrong, the criticism is correct; if you have not, the criticism is mistaken. If the criticism is correct, you have no reason to complain; if it is mistaken, it cannot do any harm to you.

4336

单则易折,众则难摧。戮力一心,然后社稷可固也。

《北史·吐谷浑传》

[英译]

Isolation is the reason for defeat whereas a united force is hard to destroy. Only when the people of a country are one in heart can its stability be ensured.

4337

与其有誉于前,孰若无毁于其后!

韩愈《送李愿归盘谷序》

[英译]

It is much better not to slander someone in his absence than to praise him when he is present.

4338

大凡君子和君子,以同道为朋;小人和小人,以同利为朋。

欧阳修《朋党论》

[英译]

Generally speaking, the friendship between superior men is on the basis of a common ideal whereas the friendship between inferior men is on the basis of mutual benefits.

4339

人之生,不幸不闻过,大不幸无耻。必有耻,则可教。闻过,则可贤。

《通书·幸》

[英译]

It is a misfortune if a person has no opportunity to hear criticism. It is a greater misfortune if a person has no self-esteem. One must have self-esteem; then one can be educated. One must listen to criticism; then one can become a worthy person.

4340

民,吾同胞;物,我与也。

《正蒙·乾称》

[英译]

All human beings are my brothers or sisters, and all creatures are my companions.

4341

天地之间,物各有主,苟非吾之所有,虽一毫而莫取。

苏轼《前赤壁赋》

[英译]

Everything between Heaven and Earth has its owner. If a thing is not mine, I will never take it, though it may be very small.

4342

忍所不能忍,容所不能容,惟识量过人者能之。

薛瑄《理学粹言》

[英译]

No one except those with extraordinary knowledge and capacity can tolerate things which are intolerable to others and accept things which are unacceptable to others.

4343

人生大病,只是一个傲字。

王阳明《传习录》

[英译]

For human beings, no disease is more serious than complacency.

4344

毋毁众人之名,以成一己之善;毋役天人之理,以护一己之过。

魏裔介《琼琚佩语》

[英译]

Do not seek to establish a good reputation for yourself by defaming others, nor to cover up your mistakes by far-fetched explanation concerning Heaven and man.

4345

忍天下之小忿者，始可以成大功；忍大辱者，始可以雪天下之大耻。

王源《居业堂文集》

[英译]

Only those who tolerate insignificant insults can achieve great success. Only those who bear great disgrace can finally wipe out the greatest humiliations.

五、智 谋 篇

Chapter 5. On Wisdom and Strategy

5346

满招损，谦受益。

《尚书・大禹谟》

［英译］

Complacency is the root of loss, and modesty is the cause of gain.

5347

师克在和，不在众。

《左传・桓公十一年》

［注释］

克：胜。

［英译］

It is the unity of a troop, not its numerical strength, that ensures victory over the enemy.

5348

夫战，勇气也。一鼓作气，再而衰，三而竭。

《左传・庄公十六年》

［英译］

Fighting is a race of courageous spirit. When the drums beat for the first round, the spirit is excited. If [the commander fails to order attack then but] waits for the second roll of drums, the spirit of the soldiers will decline. If [he still fails to order attack but] waits for the third roll of drums, the spirit will die out.

5349

皮之不存，毛将安傅？

《左传·僖公十四年》

[注释]

傅：同“附”。

[英译]

With the skin gone, where can the hair adhere?

5350

量力而动，其过鲜矣。

《左传·僖公二十年》

[英译]

To act in agreement with one's capacity, seldom will one make mistakes.

5351

允当则归。

《左传·僖公二十八年》

[注释]

允当：达到目的。

[英译]

Return as soon as the goal has been attained.

5352

有德不可敌。

《左传·僖公二十八年》

［英译］

The virtuous are unbeatable.

5353

轻则寡谋，无礼则脱。入险而脱，又不能谋，能无败乎？

《左传·僖公三十三年》

［注释］

脱：不庄重，轻率。

［英译］

Frivolity leads to a lack of strategy, and discourtesy leads to carelessness. Falling in peril without caution and strategy, how can one escape defeat?

5354

祸福无门，唯人所召。

《左传·襄公二十三年》

［英译］

Ill luck and luck do not have a fixed route of their own. They befall only in accordance with the respective deeds of people.

5355

人各有能有不能。

《左传·定公五年》

[英译]

Everyone has something he can do and something he can't do.

5356

除腹心之疾，而置之股肱，何益？

《左传·哀公六年》

[英译]

What is the benefit of shifting one's diseases of heart and belly to one's legs and arms?

5357

夫和实生物，同则不继。以他平他谓之和，故能丰长而物归之；若以同裨同，尽乃弃矣。

《国语·郑语》

[注释]

他：指不同的事物。

裨：补添。

[英译]

It is harmony that ensures the prosperous creation of things and it is sameness that may ruin them. By harmony is meant the unity of differences. Only in such conditions can things develop prosperously and can a ruler benefit from them. In contrast, the simple accumulation of things all completely the same leads to great loss.

5358

声一无听,物一无文,味一无果,物一不讲。

《国语·郑语》

[注释]

物一无文:此句中"物"意为色,文指花纹色彩。

果:美。

讲:比较。

[英译]

With just one pitch, a pretty song cannot be composed; with just one colour, a beautiful picture cannot be painted; with just one flavour, a tasty dish cannot be cooked; with things completely the same, comparison cannot be made.

5359

一年之计,莫如树谷;十年之计,莫如树木;终身之计,莫如树人。一树一获者,谷也;一树十获者,木也;一树百获者,人也。

《管子·权修》

[英译]

The best plan for one year is to cultivate grain; that for ten years is to cultivate trees; and that for a hundred years is to cultivate people. Once cultivated, grain may bring about a crop within the year; trees may bring about benefits lasting for a score of years; people may bring about benefits lasting for a hundred years.

5360

疑今者察之古,不知来者视之往。

《管子·形势》

[英译]

If you feel uncertain about something current, you may get help from history. If you do not know what is coming, you may find answers from what has passed.

5361

海不辞水,故能成其大;山不辞土石,故能成其高。

《管子·形势解》

[英译]

It is because a sea does not reject any water flowing into it that it becomes great; it is because a mountain does not reject any piece of earth or stone that it becomes high.

5362

不明于敌人之政,不能加也;不明于敌人之情,不可约也;不明于敌人之将,不先军也;不明于敌人之士,不先陈也。

《管子·七法》

[注释]

加:指出兵讨伐。

约:指做出决定。

陈:通"阵"。

[英译]

Do not launch a military expedition against an enemy country until information about its politics has been well obtained; do not make a military decision until information about enemy troops is well known; do not take military action until information about the enemy commander has been well learned; do not form a battle array until information about the enemy's formation has been well studied.

5363

知人者智，自知者明也。胜人者有力，自胜者强也。知足者富也。强行者有志也。不失其所者久也。死而不亡者寿也。

《老子》**33** 章

[**英译**]

He who knows his opponents well is wise; he who knows himself well is intelligent. He who defeats his opponents is powerful; he who defeats himself is strong. He who does not wish to transgress is wealthy. He who acts staunchly is inspiring. He who is never away from his proper position survives long. He whose spirit does not perish after his death is really long-lived.

5364

强梁者不得其死，吾将以为学父。

《老子》**42** 章

[**英译**]

The man who is arrogant and aggressive will not die a good

death, and I will take this idea as the foremost guide for my students.

5365

以正治国,以奇用兵。

《老子》57 章

[英译]

A country should be governed with overt policies and rules, whereas military actions should be carried out with covert strategies and tricks.

5366

祸兮,福之所倚;福兮,祸之所伏。

《老子》58 章

[英译]

Misfortune is the root of good fortune; good fortune gives birth to misfortune.

5367

合抱之木,生于毫末;九层之台,起于累土;千里之行,始于足下。

《老子》64 章

[英译]

A big tree was once a small seed; a nine-storey building started with a basket of earth; a journey of a thousand miles began with a first step.

5368

知不知，尚矣。不知知，病矣。夫惟病病，是以不病。圣人之不病，以其病病。

《老子》71 章

[英译]

It is salutary for one to know how little one knows, and it is morbid for one to assume that one knows what one in fact does not know. Only when one regards the morbidity as morbid can one avoid it. It is just because the sages do so that they can avoid the morbidity.

5369

天下莫柔弱于水，而攻坚强者莫之能先。以其无以易之也。柔之胜刚，弱之胜强，天下莫不知，而莫之能行。

《老子》78 章

[英译]

Water is the softest and weakest thing in the world. In penetrating hard and tough materials, however, nothing is superior to it; because nothing has the same nature to replace it. It is well known that what is weak overcomes what is strong, yet seldom can people apply it.

5370

无欲速,无见小利。欲速则不达,见小利则大事不成。

《论语·子路》

[英译]

Do not try to hurry things. Ignore petty profits. A goal cannot be attained by hurrying things. When attention is paid to petty profits, great achievements will be impossible.

5371

子不语怪力乱神。

《论语·述而》

[英译]

Confucius never spoke of magic force and unorthodox spiritual beings.

5372

暴虎冯河,死而无悔者,吾不与也。必也临事而惧,好谋而成者也。

《论语·述而》

[注释]

暴虎:徒手与猛虎搏斗。

冯河:指不用舟桥而渡河,与“暴虎”均指有勇无谋。

[英译]

Some people are ready to beard a tiger or wade the Yellow River, and they never regret it even if such actions cost their lives. I will not pick such people to accompany me in military actions. Instead, I must select people who seem to be timid before taking any action and who prefer to succeed by strategy instead of strength.

5373

子绝四:毋意,毋必,毋固,毋我。

《论语·子罕》

[注释]

意:通“臆”。

[英译]

There were four things that Confucius completely eschewed: he never made mere conjecture; he took nothing for granted; he was never simple-minded; and he was never egotistic.

5374

工欲善其事,必先利其器。

《论语·卫灵公》

[英译]

A craftsman who wants to do good work must first sharpen his tools.

5375

人无远虑,必有近忧。

《论语·卫灵公》

[英译]

He who cannot worry about what is far off will soon find troubles at hand.

5376

小不忍,则乱大谋。

《论语·卫灵公》

[英译]

Intolerance of minor insults will ruin great projects.

5377

夫战者,以正合,以奇胜。故善出奇者,无穷如天地,不竭如江河。

《孙子兵法·兵势》

[英译]

Wars are launched for overt purposes. To win them, however, needs covert or unexpected strategies. Thus, an expert of war is like Heaven, Earth, the Long River and the Yellow River, inexhaustibly creating unexpected strategies and tricks.

5378

百战百胜,非善之善者也;不战而屈人之兵,善之善者也。

《孙子兵法·谋攻》

[英译]

To have won a hundred battles is good but not the best; to force the enemy to yield without fighting is the best of all.

5379

知彼知己，百战不殆；不知彼而知己，一胜一负；不知彼不知己，每战必败。

《孙子兵法·谋攻》

［英译］

Good information of both sides promises victory over the enemy in every battle; knowing well only one's own side but knowing little of the enemy will bring an even chance to win a battle; knowing about neither side suggests the loss of every battle.

5380

善攻者，敌不知其所守，善守者，敌不知其所攻。

《孙子兵法·虚实》

［英译］

If one is really good at attack, one's enemy will have difficulties in knowing how to defend; if one is really good at defence, one's enemy will find it hard to know how to attack.

5381

投之亡地然后存，陷之死地然后生。

《孙子兵法·九地》

［英译］

An army is preserved by being put into a place without a way out [because it will then do its utmost against the enemy]; the life of a soldier is secured when he is in dire straits with no way to escape [because he will then rise to attack].

5382

故用兵之法，无恃其不来，恃吾有以待也；无恃其不攻，恃吾有所不可攻也。

《孙子兵法·九变》

［英译］

It is a rule of military action that a commander should not place hopes on the enemy's giving up advancing, but on good preparation; he should not place hopes on the enemy's ceasing to attack but on an unbroken defence.

5383

疑行无成，疑事无功。

《商君书·更法》

［英译］

He who hesitates to act can achieve nothing; he who hesitates to deal with things gains no merit.

5384

王者之兵，胜而不骄，败而不怨。胜而不骄者，术明也。败而不怨者，知所失也。

《商君书·战法》

［英译］

An army of true kingship is not arrogant about victories, nor does it complain when defeated. It is because the role of correct strategy and tactics in the victories is evident that there is no room for arrogance; it is because the reason for losing is well understood that there is no room for complaint.

5385

天时不如地利,地利不如人和。

《孟子·公孙丑下》

[英译]

[Among the factors for military victory], to act in accordance with astrological rules is not as important as to choose a favorable direction to array the troops, and to choose a favorable direction to array the troops is not as important as the unity of the generals and the soldiers.

5386

知者无不知也,当务之为急。

《孟子·尽心上》

[英译]

A wise man knows everything, but he considers urgently only the matters of top priority.

5387

瞽者无以与乎文章之观,聋者无以与乎钟鼓之声。岂唯形骸有聋盲,夫知亦有之。

《庄子·逍遥游》

[英译]

The blind get nothing from beautiful pictures, and the deaf get nothing from the tuneful play of bells and drums. Do the blind and the dead exist physically only? No, in fact, they also exist intellectually.

5388

夫水行莫如用舟，而陆行莫如用车。以舟之可行于水也而求推之于路，则没世不行寻常。

《庄子·天运》

[英译]

A boat is the best vehicle for travel on water, and a carriage is the best vehicle for travel by land. If, knowing that a boat moves well on water, one tries to push it forward on land, one will with difficulty only advance a few inches by the end of one's life.

5389

井蛙不可以语于海者，拘于虚也；夏虫不可以语冰者，笃于时也；曲士不可以语于道者，束于教也。

《庄子·秋水》

[英译]

With a frog who never leaves the well one cannot discuss the ocean, because of spatial limitations; with a worm who does not survive summer, one can not discuss snow, because of temporal limitations. Similarly, with a shallow scholar one cannot discuss the Great Tao because of the limitations of the dogma he learned.

5390

褚小者不可以怀大,绠短者不可以汲深。

《庄子·至乐》

[注释]

褚:衣袋。

绠:井绳。

[英译]

A small pocket cannot contain big things; with a short well-rope, one cannot draw water from a deep well.

5391

以隋侯之珠,弹千仞之雀,世必笑之。是何也?则其所用者重,而所要者轻也。

《庄子·让王》

[注释]

隋侯之珠:古代传说中的明珠。

[英译]

If one shoots a valuable pearl at a sparrow flying high in the sky, the whole world will laugh at one. Why? Because what one spends is too precious and what one expects to gain is too trivial.

5392

知者之举事也,满则虑嗛,平则虑险,安则虑危,曲重其豫,犹恐及其祸,是以百举而不陷也。

《荀子·仲尼》

[注释]

嗛:通“谦”。

豫:忧虑。

[英译]

A man of wisdom is very cautious in taking action. He keeps modesty in mind when he enjoys satisfaction; he keeps difficulties in mind when the action develops smoothly; he keeps perils in mind when he is at ease. Although he is already very cautious, yet he still worries about the possibility of unexpected misfortune. In so doing, he will lose no-one in a hundred actions.

5393

物固莫不有长,莫不有短。人亦然。故善学者,假人之长以补其短。

《吕氏春秋·用众》

[英译]

Everything has both strong points and shortcomings. So does every human being. Therefore, he who is good at learning always takes advantage of others' strong points to make up for his own shortcomings.

5394

夫有以噎死者,欲禁天下之食,悖。有以乘舟死者,欲禁天下之船,悖。有以用兵丧国者,欲偃天下之兵,悖。夫兵不可偃也,譬之若水火然,善用之则为福,不能用之则为祸。若用药者然,得良药则活人,得恶药则杀人。

《吕氏春秋·荡兵》

[注释]

偃:废止。

[英译]

It is obviously absurd to abolish meals just because some people were choked to death when eating, and it is also absurd to ban boats just because some people were drowned when travelling by boat. It is equally absurd to abolish military forces only because some people ruined their countries in military actions. Military forces should by no means be abolished. The application of military forces is similar to the use of water and fire. People will benefit from correctly using them but they will suffer disasters by incorrectly using them. It is also similar to the application of medicine. Taking correctly prescribed medicine may save one's life, but taking incorrectly prescribed medicine may kill one.

5395

有道之士,贵以近知远,以今知古,以所见知所不见。

《吕氏春秋·察今》

[英译]

A man of Tao values to know the far through the near, to know the ancient through the present, and to know the hidden through the seen.

5396

流水不腐，户枢不蝼。

《吕氏春秋·尽数》

［注释］

蝼：虫蛀。

［英译］

Flowing water does not go foul, and a moving arrow-shaft does not get worm-eaten.

5397

知之难，不在见人，在自见。

《韩非子·解老》

［英译］

What is difficult to know is not someone else but oneself.

5398

千丈之堤，以蝼蚁之穴溃；百尺之室，以突隙之烟焚。

《韩非子·喻老》

［注释］

突隙：烟道。

［英译］

A huge dike may collapse just through ant holes; a huge building may burn out just because of a spark from a chimney's chink.

5399

削株掘根，无与祸邻，祸乃不存。

《战国策·秦策》

[英译]

If one can eliminate the main causes of perils, wipe out their roots, and keep away from them, the perils will no longer take place.

5400

以乱攻治者亡，以邪攻正者亡，以逆攻顺者亡。

《战国策·秦策》

[英译]

When a chaotic country attacks a stable one, the former will inevitably meet its doom; when an evil country attacks a just one, the former will inevitably meet its doom; when a perverse country attacks a proper one, the former will inevitably meet its doom.

5401

计者，事之本也；听者，存亡之机。计失而听过，能有国者寡也。

《战国策·秦策》

[英译]

Success of political affairs is based upon correct strategies, and the ups and downs of a country depend on the attitude of its ruler towards varied advice. If the ruler fails to take correct strategies and accepts wrong advice, seldom can he secure his power.

5402

日中则移，月满则亏，物盛则衰，天之常数也；进退、盈缩、变化，圣人之常道也。

《战国策·秦策》

[英译]

It is the general order of Heaven that the sun will decline as soon as it reaches the meridian, that the moon is going to wane as soon as it waxes to full, and that things go down as soon as their zenith is reached. Resembling the order of Heaven, the Tao of sages carefully considers advances and withdraws, expansion and contraction and change and transformation.

5403

谋泄者事无功，计不决者名不成。

《战国策·齐策》

[英译]

He who fails to keep his plan secret will achieve nothing; he who fails to make decisions in due time gains no reputation.

5404

猿猕猴错木据水，则不若鱼鳖；历险乘危，则骐骥不如狐狸。曹沫奋三尺之剑，一军不能当；使曹沫释其三尺之剑，而操铫耨与农夫居陇亩之中，则不若农夫。故物舍其所长，之其所短，尧亦有所不及矣。

《战国策·齐策》

[注释]

错:放弃。

曹沫:古代传说中善剑者。

铫耨:除草具。

[英译]

A monkey who leaves the trees and swims in the water is inferior to a fish. A famous race-horse, when put in dangerous and complex environment, is inferior to a fox. Cao Mo, a famous swordsman whose technique is so excellent that thousands of soldiers cannot beat him, is inferior to a peasant when his sword is replaced by a hoe and he is ordered to cultivate grain. Even such a sage as Yao would be at his wits' end if he had to renounce his talents and play an unfamiliar role.

5405

效小节者不能行大威,恶小耻者不能立荣名。

《战国策·齐策》

[英译]

He who cares too much about trivial manners will never achieve great dignity. He who is intolerable of minor insults will never establish a glorious reputation.

5406

夫物多相类而非也,幽莠之幼也似禾,骊牛之黄也似虎,白骨疑象,武夫类玉,此皆似之而非者也。

《战国策·魏策》

[注释]

幽莠:狗尾草。

骊牛:黑黄色的牛

白骨疑象:白骨与象牙类似。

武夫:一种似玉之石。

[英译]

There are many cases of two things looking alike but being different in nature. Bristlegrass looks like crops when young; a black-and-yellow-coloured ox looks like a tiger from afar; a piece of white bone looks like ivory; and a piece of Wu Fu stone looks like jade. All these are examples of things seemingly the same but different in nature.

5407

将欲败之,必先辅之;将欲取之,必先与之。

《战国策·魏策》

[英译]

If you want to ruin your foe, you must first offer him help to make him relax; if you want to deprive someone of his powers, you must first increase his power to make him relax.

5408

夫无谋人之心,而令人疑之,殆;有谋人之心,而令人知之,拙;谋未发而闻于外,则危。

《战国策·燕策》

[英译]

It is foolhardy for one who does not intend to plot against others to lay himself open to suspicion of plotting; it is hazardous for one who does intend to plot against others to let them know it; it is deadly for one who has not yet started the plot to reveal it to the public.

5409

善作者,不必善成;善始者,不必善终。

《战国策·燕策》

[英译]

Those who are good at initiating something are not necessarily those who are good at accomplishing it; those who are good at starting are not necessarily those who are good at finishing.

5410

当断不断,反受其乱。

《十六经·观》

[英译]

If the time for making a decision comes but a person is reluctant to make it, he will suffer misfortune caused by his hesitation.

5411

制人反失其理,反制焉。

《称》

[英译]

He who tries to control others but fails to do it in accord with the principles will be controlled by others.

5412

两虎相争，奴犬制其余。

《称》

[注释]

奴犬：劣狗。

余：指相争后的幸存者。

[英译]

After a ferocious fight to the death between two tigers, a common dog may defeat the survivor.

5413

非计策无以决嫌定疑，非谲奇无以破奸息寇，非计谋无以成功。

《黄石公三略·中略》

[注释]

谲：变化多端。

[英译]

Nothing but correct policy can remove one's hesitation in military affairs; nothing but tactics and tricks can ruin the enemy and beat the rebellion; nothing but excellent strategy can secure success.

5414

长莫长于博谋，孤莫孤于自恃。

《素书》

[英译]

The best merit is simply wide consultations with others; the most isolated person is the man who is of extremely self-assured.

5415

浴不必江海，要之去垢；马不必骐骥，要之善走。

《史记·外戚世家》

[英译]

Seeking a place to bathe, one does not necessarily choose the sea or a great river but anywhere as long as the dirt can be removed. Seeking a horse to ride, one does not necessarily choose a famous one but any horse as long as it can run well.

5416

反听之谓聪，内视之谓明，自胜之谓强。

《史记·商君列传》

[英译]

A person is a good hearer if he listens inwardly to himself; a good seer if he looks into himself; a strong man if he overcomes himself.

5417

鉴于水者见面之容,鉴于人者知吉与凶。

《史记·范雎蔡泽列传》

[英译]

With water as a mirror, one can see one's facial features. With people as mirrors, one may know whether one will have good or ill fortune.

5418

智者千虑,必有一失。愚者千虑,必有一得。

《史记·淮阴侯列传》

[英译]

Among a thousand ideas of a wise man, there will certainly be at least one which is mistaken; among a thousand ideas of a stupid man, there will certainly be at least one which is a truth.

5419

盖明者远见于未萌,而知者避危于无形,祸固多藏于隐微而发于人之所忽者也。故鄙谚曰:"家累千金,坐不垂堂"。此言虽小,可以喻大。

《史记·司马相如列传》

[注释]

垂堂:靠近屋檐处,有被掉下来的瓦片砸伤的危险。

[英译]

A man of intelligence may foresee the future development of a hidden sprout; a man of wisdom may avoid the perils in their formless beginning. Disasters are often hidden in a formless state and arise due to the ignorance of people. Therefore, as a folk song goes: "If you have accumulated a thousand pounds in gold, you'd better avoid sitting under unstable eaves". Although this folk song refers to trivial things, yet its meaning may be applied to significant matters.

5420

失之豪厘,差以千里。

《史记·太史公自序》

[注释]

豪:通“毫”。

[英译]

An error as small as a single hair can lead you a thousand miles off course.

5421

通一孔,晓一理,而不知权衡,以所不睹不信人,若蝉之不知雪。

桓宽《盐铁论·相刺》

[英译]

A man who only knows a small part of a huge thing, who only knows a minor principle without comparing it with others, and who questions the existence of things mentioned by others only because he has not yet seen it himself, is like a cicada that cannot understand snow.

5422

高议而不可及，不若卑论之有功也。

《说苑·说丛》

[英译]

Lofty but impractical comments are not as good as humble but practical ones.

5423

小辩害大知，巧言使信废，小惠妨大义。不固在于早虑，不穷在于早豫。

《说苑·说丛》

[英译]

Trivial dispute is harmful to high intelligence; cunning remarks ruin trust; and petty perks are detrimental to great righteousness. On the contrary, foresight removes difficulties, and precaution avoids exhaustion.

5424

谋先事则昌，事先谋则亡。

《说苑·说丛》

[英译]

To plan before taking action foretells success, and to take action before planning suggests destruction.

5425

智者不妄为，勇者不妄杀。

《说苑·说丛》

[英译]

A man of wisdom does not act presumptuously, and a man of courage does not kill casually.

5426

善师者不陈，善陈者不战，善战者不败，善败者不亡。

《汉书·刑法志》

[注释]

陈：通"阵"。

[英译]

He who is really good at military actions never draws up a battle formation; he who is really good at drawing up a battle formation never seeks a battle; he who is really good at fighting never loses battles; he who is really good at reviving from being defeated never causes his army to die out.

5427

临渊羡鱼，不如退而结网。

《汉书·董仲舒传》

[英译]

To covet fish while standing at a lake with bare hands is not as useful as to go away and weave a net.

5428

反复参考,无以先入之语为主。

《汉书·息夫躬传》

[英译]

Think matters over and over, making careful comparisons, and do not make a pre-judgement in favour of what is heard first.

5429

先发制人,后发制于人。

《汉书·项籍传》

[英译]

Taking the initiative leads to firm control over the enemy, whereas passive responses lead to one's being controlled by the enemy.

5430

不入虎穴,不得虎子。

《后汉书·班超传》

[英译]

How can you catch tiger cubs without entering the tiger's lair?

5431

智者弃其所短,而采其所长,以致其功。

《潜夫论·实质》

[英译]

A wise man will stress other people's strong points in order to overcome their shortcomings.

5432

势盛必衰,形露必败,故能因敌变化,取胜者神。

曹操《孙子注·虚实》

[英译]

What is at its peak is certain to decline, and those who reveal the direction of their actions are certain to lose. Therefore, he who can win the battle by taking advantage of the vicissitudes of the enemy is the most admirable general.

5433

一年之计在于春,一日之计在于晨。

萧绎《纂要》

[英译]

The whole year's work depends on a good start in the spring; a whole day's work depends on a good start in the morning.

5434

夫曲思于细者,必忘其大。锐精于近者,必略于远。由心不并驻,则事不兼通。小有所系,大必所忘也。

《刘子·观量》

[英译]

He who pays too much attention to detail will surely neglect major problems. He who makes too much effort on matters at hand is sure to fail to make plans for the future. Why? Because a single mind cannot concentrate on two matters at once and it cannot pay equal attention to different things. Since it is dealing with trivial things, the great ones are bound to be neglected.

5435

才能成功,以速为贵;智能决谋,以疾为奇也。善济事者,若救水拯溺。明其谋者,犹骥捷矢疾。

《刘子·贵速》

[英译]

Among talented people, those who achieve quick successes are the most valuable; among the wise, those who can make prompt decisions are the most excellent. He who is good at achieving acts as swiftly as if he were saving a drowning man. He who is good at carrying out a strategy responds to developments as speedily as a galloping horse or a flying arrow.

5436

智所以为妙者,以其应时而知,若事过而后知,则与无知者齐矣。

《刘子·贵速》

[英译]

The reason why a man of wisdom is wonderful and excellent lies in his ability to know things on time. Suppose he knew a thing only after it had already passed, he would be no different from those who do not know things.

5437

万人离心,不如百人同力;千人递战,不如十人俱至。

《刘子·兵术》

[注释]

递:依次。

[英译]

An army of ten thousand soldiers, each differing in mind from the next man is inferior to an army of only a hundred soldiers who are all of one mind. A thousand soldiers fighting one after another against the enemy is not as effective as only a score of them fighting the enemy simutaneously.

5438

挽弓当挽强,用箭当用长。射人先射马,擒贼先擒王。

杜甫《前出塞》

[英译]

Use the bow which is hard to bend, and the arrows of greatest length. Shoot the enemy's horse rather than the rider; and the best tactic is to capture first the enemy's leader.

5439

沉舟侧畔千帆过,病树前头万木春。

刘禹锡《酬乐天扬州初逢席上见赠》

［英译］

Ten thousand ships sail ahead over a sunken one, and by a withered trunk ten thousand trees flourish in the spring.

5440

夫祸患常积于忽微，而智勇多困于所溺。

欧阳修《五代史·伶官传序》

［英译］

Disasters often befall through the accumulation of insignificant things; hardships hit the wise and brave mainly through their addictions.

5441

为将之道，当先治心。泰山崩于前而色不变，麋鹿兴于左而目不瞬，然后可以制利害，可以待敌。

苏洵《心术》

［英译］

Psychological training is a prerequisite for a general. Only when he would not be frightened even if Mount Tai collapsed before him and he would not blink even though a deer suddenly jumped out at him, could such a general clearly distinguish gains from losses, and be qualified to lead an army against the enemy.

5442

凡主将之道，知理而后可以举兵，知势而后可以加兵，知节而后可以用兵。知理则不屈，知势则不沮，知节则不穷。

苏洵《心术》

[英译]

For the Tao of training a commander, it is only after a man knows principles that can he call upon the army; it is only after he knows the tendency that can he direct the army; and it is only after he knows moderation that can he order the army into battle. Knowing principles, he will not yield; knowing the tendency, he will not be frustrated; knowing moderation, he will not be exhausted.

5443

善用兵者，使之无所顾，有所恃。无所顾，则知死亡不足惜；有所恃，则知不至于必败。

苏洵《心术》

[英译]

An excellent commander will leave his soldiers with no doubts, but give them clear directions. With no doubts, they will not hesitate to risk their lives in battle; with clear directions to follow, they will know that defeat is not unavoidable.

5444

夫天下将治，则人必尚行也；天下将乱，则人必尚言也。尚行则笃实之风行焉，尚言则诡谲之风行焉。

邵雍《皇极经世书》

[英译]

People preferring action rather than speech indicates with certainty that a time of stability is coming; on the contrary, people's preference for speech over action indicates with certainty that a time of chaos is coming. When action is preferred, the customs of honesty and sincerity will prevail; when speech is preferred, customs of hypocrisy and trickery will prevail.

5445

夫君子之所取者远,则必有所待;所就者大,则必有所忍。

苏轼《贾谊论》

[英译]

Since a long way lies ahead for a gentleman to achieve great success, he must be patient with preparation; since his final aim is grand, he must tolerate trivial insults.

5446

横看成岭侧成峰,远近高低各不同。不识庐山真面目,只缘身在此山中。

苏轼《题西林壁》

[英译]

Looking at the same object from different points, one may get different views. One may fail to grasp the real appearance of Mount Lu merely because one is looking at it while climbing the mountain.

5447

用兵之道,形与势二。不知而一之,则沮于形,眩于势,而胜不可图,且坐受其毙矣。何谓形?小大是也。何谓势?虚实是也。

辛弃疾《美芹十论·审势》

[英译]

According to the right Tao of military action, form and situation are two things. Those who regard them as one will get confused about the two things. They will not only lack hope for victory over enemy, but simply lead themselves to their own doom. What is form? It refers to the size of things. What is situation? It refers to the strength of things.

5448

阵而后战,兵法之常,运用之妙,存乎一心。

《宋史·岳飞传》

[英译]

It is common knowledge in military arts that an army should not fight till a battle formation has been set up. As for the best application of the military arts to a real battle, it depends on the wisdom of the commander.

5449

夫兵不患寡,患骄慢而不精;将不患怯,患偏见而无谋。

《宋史·何继筠传》

[英译]

What soldiers need to worry about is not that they are numerically inferior to the enemy, but that they are complacent and not well trained; what generals need to worry about is not that they are not brave enough, but that they are subjective and do not have strategic insight.

5450

盖闻蠖屈求伸,非终于屈;龙潜或跃,非固于潜。是故勾践事吴,乃成姑苏之举;夷吾佐霸,曷问槛车之嫌。

《诚意伯刘文成公文集·拟连珠》

[注释]

蠖:尺蠖虫。

姑苏之举:指越王勾践攻灭吴王夫差于姑苏。

夷吾:即管仲。

槛车之嫌:指管仲曾与齐桓公为仇,射伤齐桓公后被囚之事。

[英译]

When moving, a caterpillar will contract and expand in turn. It has to contract for a while but does not contract for ever. A dragon in action will hide itself under water for a while and jump out to fly for another. It has to hide itself in water for a while but does not stay under water for ever. Therefore, Gou Jian, a king of Yue, once turned himself into a servant of the King of Wu and finally eliminated Wu; Guan Zhong, who assisted Duke Huan of Qi to achieve lordship, never minded that he had once been the prisoner of the duke.

5451

盖闻志大业者，必择所任；抱大器者，必择所投。是以梁江湖，不取螬残之木；钓鲸鲵，不适雨盈之沟。

《诚意伯刘文成公文集·拟连珠》

［注释］

梁：架桥。

［英译］

A ruler who aims at good government must carefully choose his ministers; those with great aspirations must carefully choose the right ruler to serve. To build bridges across big rivers or lakes one does not use worm-eaten timber; to fish for whales one does not go to small ditches.

5452

显者示以晦之理，则闷；浅者动以深之机，则迷；愚者诏以智之谋，则惑。人各有至，不可强也。

王廷相《慎言·小宗》

［英译］

When a man who can only understand the obvious principles is told something obscure, he will find it difficult; when a shallow man is told something profound, he will be puzzled; when a stupid man is told something very wise, he will be confused. People have their limitations: it is folly to try to force them to understand what is beyond their comprehension.

5453

好问好察，改过不吝之谓上智；饰非拒谏，自以为是之谓下愚。故上智者必不自智，下愚者必不自愚。下愚必自以为聪明才智之人。

《陈确集·瞀言》

［英译］

A man who is fond of consulting others, likes investigating things and corrects his own mistakes is called a man of highest wisdom. He who covers up his mistakes, rejects criticism and is conceited is called a man of the greatest stupidity. Therefore, a man of highest wisdom will certainly not consider himself wise, whereas a man of the greatest stupidity will certainly not consider himself stupid. Instead, the latter regards himself as a man of wisdom and intelligence.

5454

好胜者必败，恃壮者易疾。

魏裔介《琼琚佩语》

［英译］

He who seeks nothing but to do others down will inevitably suffer defeat; he who relies on nothing but his physical strength will easily meet with troubles.

5455

用兵者，无时非危，故无时不谨。入军如有侦，出境俨临交，获取验无害，遇阻必索奸，敌来虑有谋，我出必预计，慎以行师，至道也。

《皇朝经世文编》

［英译］

In military actions, there is no time without peril. Therefore, vigilance is always necessary. When a general stays with his army, he should feel as if he were out scouting. When he enters enemy territory, he should feel as if a serious battle will break out immediately. When he captures anything from the enemy, he must examine it for hidden trickery. When he encounters difficulties, he must check if there are spies concealed in his army. When the enemy challenges, he must think over whether or not it is a plot. Before he orders attack, he must make good preparations with correct strategy. It is the best way for military action to stay cautious.

5456

大凡用计者，非一计之可孤行，必有数计以襄之也。

《皇朝经世文编》

［注释］

襄：助。

［英译］

To secure victory over the enemy, a single strategem is far from enough. There must be a series of strategems to assist a major one.

5457

天下事当于大处著眼，小处下手。

曾国藩《曾文正公全集》

［英译］

Dealing with things, we must have a comprehensive picture of the whole but begin with a small part in detail.

六、为 政 篇

Chapter 6.　On Government

6458

君子安而不忘危，存而不忘亡，治而不忘乱。

《易·系辞下》

［英译］

A superior man, when resting in safety, does not forget that danger may come; when in a state of security, he does not forget the possibility of ruin; and when his country is in a state of order, he does not forget that disorder may come.

6459

天聪明，自我民聪明；天明畏，自我民明威。

《尚书·皋陶谟》

［英译］

It is through the hearing and sight of the people that Heaven hears and sees; it is through the display of the people's awesome power that Heaven issues its warning.

6460

民惟邦本，本固邦宁。

《尚书·五子之歌》

［英译］

People are the foundation of a country. When the foundation is stable, the country is in peace.

6461

内作色荒，外作禽荒，甘酒嗜音，峻宇雕墙；有一于此，未或不亡。

《尚书·五子之歌》

[英译]

A ruler who indulges himself with domestic beauty or with hunting outdoors, who is obsessed with wine and music, who builds lofty, ornate palaces—a ruler engaged in any of these things will never be able to avoid the ruin of his country.

6462

德日新，万邦惟怀；志自满，九族乃离。

《尚书·仲虺之诰》

[英译]

When a ruler improves his morality day by day, all the countries under Heaven will pay reverence to him. If he is complacent, even his relatives will leave him.

6463

能自得师者王，谓人莫己若者亡。

《尚书·仲虺之诰》

[英译]

When a ruler is able to find teachers to learn from, he is going to attain true kingship; if he considers others inferior to himself, he is going to meet his doom.

6464

有言逆于汝心，必求诸道；有言逊于汝心，必求诸非道。

《尚书·太甲》

[注释]

逊：顺。

[英译]

When there is a speech with which you disagree, you must examine whether it is in accordance with Tao; when there is a speech with which you agree, you must examine whether it is in discordance with Tao.

6465

任官惟贤才。

《尚书·咸有一德》

[英译]

Nobody but those of excellent morality and capacity should be appointed to official posts.

6466

树德务滋，除恶务本。

《尚书·泰誓》

[英译]

When you plant virtue, strive to make it sturdy; when you remove wickedness, strive to do it from the roots.

6467

八政：一曰食，二曰货，三曰礼，四曰司空，五曰司徒，六曰司寇，七曰宾，八曰师。

《尚书·洪范》

[注释]

司空、司徒、司寇：古官名，分管工程，徒役，防盗等事务。

[英译]

The eight [concerns of] government are as follow: The first is food; the second, wealth; the third, rites; the fourth, the [business] of the Minister of Construction; the fifth, [that] of the Minister of Labour; the sixth, [that of] the Minister of Crime; the seventh, [that of] the Minister of Foreign Affairs; and the eighth, the army.

6468

张而不弛，文武弗能也；弛而不张，文武弗为也。一张一弛，文武之道也。

《礼记·杂记》

[英译]

Even the Kings Wen and Wu could not remain tense without any relaxation. Neither would they allow themselves relaxation without tension. To be alternately strung and unstrung was the Tao they followed.

6469

大道之行也，天下为公。选贤与能，讲信修睦。故人不独亲其亲，不独子其子，使老有所终，壮有所用，幼有所长，矜寡孤独废疾者，皆有所养。男有分，女有归。货恶其弃于地也，不必藏于己。力恶其不出于身也，不必为己。是故谋闭而不兴，盗窃乱贼而不作，故外户而不闭，是谓大同。

《礼记·礼运》

[**注释**]

矜寡：同“鳏寡”。

[**英译**]

When the Great Tao prevailed, public spiritedness ruled all the world. Then nobody was promoted but those of worth and talent. No doctrines were taught but those of sincerity and harmony, and they were followed in moral cultivation. Thus men did not love only their own parents or treat as their children only their own sons. A life-long provision was made for the aged; employment was found for the able-bodied and, for the young, an environment in which they could mature. Widows, orphans, childless men and those disabled by disease were all given sufficient maintenance. Males had their proper work, and females their homes. They did not like to throw things away on the ground but kept them, not necessarily for their gratification so that they might share them with others. They did not happily enjoy things which they had not paid for by their own efforts, but did not work simply for their own good. Therefore exploitation was suppressed. There were no robbers, tricksters, rebels or traitors. The outer doors remained opened. This is what was meant by the "Great Unification".

6470

亲人善邻,国之宝也。

《左传·隐公六年》

［英译］

Love of the people and kindness to neighbouring countries—these are the treasures of a nation.

6471

长恶不悛,从自及也。虽欲救之,其将能乎?

《左传·隐公六年》

［注释］

悛:改过。

［英译］

When evil is done without any attempt at correction, it harms the doer himself. Once disaster befalls him, can he still have the opportunity to restore the situation, even if he wants to?

6472

禹汤罪己,其兴也悖焉;桀纣罪人,其亡也忽焉。

《左传·庄公十一年》

［注释］

悖:通"勃",迅速。

忽:迅速。

[英译]

When they had done something wrong, Kings Yu and Tang would undertake self-criticism, and this was the reason why the countries they had just founded rose suddenly. In the same situation, Kings Jie and Zhou blamed others in stead of criticising themselves, and this was the reason why their countries declined abruptly.

6473

国将兴,听于民;将亡,听于神。

《左传·庄公三十二年》

[英译]

It is an omen for the rise of a country that its ruler listens to the advice of the people; it is an omen for the decline of a country that its ruler listens only to the diviners.

6474

皇天无亲,唯德是辅。

《左传·僖公五年》

[注释]

辅:助。

[英译]

The Celestial Being favours nobody, and it helps only those of virtue.

6475

弃信背邻，患孰恤之？无信患作，失援必毙。

《左传·僖公十四年》

［英译］

Who on earth can pity one who is unable to keep his word and breaks faith with his neighbours? Disasters will certainly befall when one cannot keep his word, and he will certainly meet his doom without the help of others.

6476

弃德崇奸，祸之大者也。

《左传·僖公二十四年》

［英译］

It is the greatest disaster to abandon virtues and to favour evils.

6477

信，国之宝也，民之所庇也。

《左传·僖公二十五年》

［英译］

Sincerity is the treasure of a country and it is by sincerity that people find their shelter.

6478

敬，德之聚也。能敬必有德，德以治民。

《左传·僖公三十三年》

[英译]

Reverence is at the centre of the various virtues. He who can pay reverence to others is necessarily a man of virtue and to be virtuous is the very means of government.

6479

践修旧好,要结外援,好事邻国,以卫社稷。忠信,卑让之道也。忠,德之正也;信,德之固也;卑让,德之基也。

《左传·文公元年》

[英译]

It is necessary for the security of a country to restore and further old friendships, to form alliances, thereby seeking external supports, and to keep good relations with all neighbouring countries. It is the Tao of loyalty, sincerity, and modesty. Loyalty is the centre of virtues, sincerity their consolidator and modesty their foundation.

6480

叛而不讨,何以示威?服而不柔,何以示怀?非威非怀,何以示德?

《左传·文公七年》

[英译]

If a ruler does not punish his betrayers, how can he show dignity? If he does no favours to those who obey him, how can he show kindness? Without dignity and kindness, how can he show his virtues?

6481

民生在勤，勤则不匮。

《左传·宣公十二年》

[英译]

Livelihood depends on diligence. People will never suffer poverty when they work hard.

6482

众怒难犯，专欲难成；合二以安国，危之道也。

《左传·襄公十一年》

[英译]

A ruler will certainly meet difficulties if he angers the multitude and he can hardly be fulfiled if he seeks to make a profit by means of monopolies. If he manages to do both at the same time, pretending that it is for the security of his country, he is in fact going to ruin it.

6483

居安思危，思则有备，有备无患，敢以此规。

《左传·襄公十一年》

[英译]

By staying vigilant against possible dangers, one will be prepared against them. When one is prepared for them, the troubles will not come about. I venture this as a precept.

6484

宋人或得宝,献诸子罕。子罕弗受。献玉者曰:“以示玉人,玉人以为宝也,故敢献之。”子罕曰:“我以不贪为宝,尔以玉为宝,若以与我,皆丧宝也,不若人有其宝。”

《左传·襄公十五年》

[英译]

A man of the State of Song happened to find a piece of jade and presented it as a gift to Zi Han, the chief minister of that state. When the latter refused to accept it, the man explained: "I have shown it to a jeweler and he guaranteed its value. Only then did I dare offer it to your excellency." Zi Han replied, "I value not being greedy whereas you value jade. If I should accept your gift, we should each lose what we value. We had better both keep what we have."

6485

大上有立德,其次有立功,其次有立言。虽久不废,此之谓不朽。

《左传·襄公二十四年》

[英译]

It is best to establish great virtue; second best is to achieve great things; third best is to create great literature. These three things last undestroyed for a long time, and those who have established them can last forever.

6486

政如农功，日夜思之，思其始而成其终，朝夕而行之。行无越思，如农之有畔，其过鲜也。

《左传·襄公二十五年》

［英译］

Government is akin to farming. One must pay constant attention to both; both require good planning from the start; both require measures to ensure that the tasks will be completed successfully. The ruler must work every day to avoid infringing the rules which apply to his task, just as the farmer must avoid destroying the ridges. If he does, he will seldom make mistakes.

6487

善为国者，赏不僭而刑不滥。赏僭则惧及淫人，刑滥则惧及善人。

《左传·襄公二十六年》

［英译］

A skillful ruler avoids both excessive awards and excessive penalties, because he is afraid that excessive awards will be given to the wicked, and that excessive penalties will be given to the good.

6488

君子务在择人。

《左传·襄公二十九年》

［英译］

A superior man manages to choose the right men to charge

with official posts.

6489

我闻忠善以损怨,不闻作威以防怨。岂不遽止?然犹防川,大决所犯,伤人必多,吾不克救也。不如小决,使道,不如吾闻而药之也。

《左传·襄公三十年》

[英译]

I heard that one should lessen others' resentment against him by being loyal and kind to them, and it is impossible to avoid others' resentment by being awful and ferocious. It is true that such measures may temporarily stop criticism. Like building a dam to stop a river, however, a great collapse will take place with heavy casualties, and there will be no way for restoration. For water projects, it is better to dredge rivers in order that the water can flow smoothly. For government, a ruler had better take criticism against him as a medicine.

6490

安定国家,必大焉先。

《左传·襄公三十年》

[英译]

To stabilise a country, top priority must be given to the most significant matters.

6491

为政者不赏私劳，不罚私怨。

《左传·昭公五年》

［英译］

Men in power should not confer rewards in return for personal favour, or punish those who speak out against them.

6492

政不可不慎也。务三而已：一曰择人，二曰因民，三曰从时。

《左传·昭公七年》

［英译］

A ruler cannot but be very cautious in government and he must devote himself to these three matters: choice of the right men as ministers, adherence to the will of the people, the planning and timing of his actions.

6493

好恶不愆，民知所适，事无不济。

《左传·昭公十五年》

［英译］

When good deeds are rewarded and evil ones are punished without exception, people will surely know which to emulate and they will accomplish all that the ruler orders.

6494

政宽则民慢，慢则纠之以猛。猛则民残，残则施之以宽。宽以济猛，猛以济宽，政是以和。

《左传·昭公二十年》

[英译]

With a liberal government, people will become undisciplined. Then the cure is to make the government more severe. With a severe government, people will be harmed. Then the cure is to liberalise the government. The liberal and the severe supplement each other. In this way, a government becomes well balanced.

6495

唯有德者能以宽服民，其次莫如猛。夫火烈，民望而畏之，故鲜死焉。水懦弱，民狎而玩之，则多死焉。故宽难。

《左传·昭公二十年》

[英译]

Only a ruler of virtue is able to make people obedient to him with a liberal government. A comparison may be made with the severe ruler. Fire is fierce, and people fear at the sight of it. So they seldom die of it. Water, on the other hand, is gentle, so that people are inclined to play in it. As a result, many of them drown. For this reason we say that it is very difficult to have a liberal but successful government.

6496

夫恃才与众，亡之道也。商纣由之，故灭。

《左传·宣公十五年》

[英译]

One shouldn't rely on numerical superiority or rely on one's wits, or this will lead to destruction. The King Zhou of the Shang did so, and he thereby ruined himself.

6497

防民之口,甚于防川。川壅而溃,伤人必多,民亦如之。是故为川者决之使导,为民者宣之使言。

《国语·周语》

[英译]

To forbid people's criticism is more dangerous than to dam a river. The obstructed water will certainly burst with the collapse of the dam, and many will be killed as a result. To stop people criticising will result in the same. Therefore, a successful hydraulic engineer will dredge rivers instead of damming them, and a successful ruler will encourage his people to speak out.

6498

夫民虑之于心,而宣之于口,成而行之,胡可壅也?若雍其口,其与能几何?

《国语·周语》

[英译]

When people have something in mind, they will speak it out and then put it into practice. How can they be prohibited from speaking? If a ruler tries to do this, how long can his prohibition last?

6499

不厚其栋，不能任重。

《国语·鲁语》

［英译］

Without strengthening one's shoulder, one cannot be charged with a significant duty.

6500

少德而多宠，位下而欲上政，无大功而欲大禄，皆怨府也。

《国语·鲁语》

［英译］

Inferior in virtue but enjoying much favour; ranking low but intervening in state affairs; achieving no great success but seeking the highest salary; all these are the sources of hatred.

6501

伐木不自其本，必复生；塞水不自其源，必复流；灭祸不自其基，必复乱。

《国语·晋语》

［英译］

With its root remaining, the regrowth of a lopped tree will be unavoidable. With its source remaining, the restoration of obstructed water will be unavoidable. With its basis remaining, a disaster which has temporarily disappeared will surely reappear.

6502

夫正国者,不可以昵于权,行权不可以隐于私。昵于权,则民不导;行权隐于私,则政不行。

《国语·晋语》

[英译]

To establish a well-ordered government, a ruler cannot indulge in expedient measures. When expedient measures have to be performed, he cannot do it to meet private need. If he indulges in expedient measures, he will not be able to lead his people; if he meets his private need when expedient measures have to be performed, his orders cannot be carried out.

6503

口不贪嘉味,耳不乐逸声,目不淫于色,身不怀于安,朝夕勤志,恤民之羸,闻一善若惊,得一士若赏,有过必悛,有不善必惧,是故得民以济其志。

《国语·楚语》

[注释]

羸:弱。

悛:悔改。

[英译]

A ruler should not be greedy for luxurious food, enjoy frivolous music, or give his attention to sexual attraction. He should pursue his ideal with diligence, caring greatly for the weak and disabled among the people. When he learns of something good he should feel special pleasure and the discovery of a talented individual should please him as much as if he were himself to receive some honour. He should correct his mistakes and fear error. In this way a ruler wins the support of the people and will finally achieve his objectives.

6504

量民力,则事无不成;不强民以其所恶,则诈伪不生。

《管子·牧民》

[英译]

If he gives full consideration to the capacity of people, a ruler may achieve any objective. If he avoids constraining people to act against their wishes, he will not be cheated by hypocricy or lies.

6505

政之所行,在顺民心。政之所废,在逆民心。

《管子·牧民》

[英译]

The efficiency of a government depends on its sympathy with public opinion; its failure often results from its antagonism to public opinion.

6506

国多财则远者来,地辟举则民留处;仓禀实则知礼节,衣食足则知荣辱。

《管子·牧民》

[注释]

举:发展。

[英译]

When a country abunds in wealth, strangers will immigrate to it. When there is plenty of land to farm, people will no longer expect to emigrate. When there are adequate stores, people will know the right way to behave themselves. When people have enough clothing and food, they will know the difference between right and wrong.

6507

有德义未明于朝者,则不可加于尊位;功力未见于国者,则不可援以重禄;临事不信于民者,则不可使任大官。故德厚而位卑者谓之过,德薄而位尊者谓之失。宁过于君子,而毋失于小人。

《管子·立政》

[英译]

Do not confer lofty titles to those who are not yet well known for their virtue and righteousness. Do not give generous salaries to those who have not yet achieved nationwide success. Do not offer high posts to those who have not yet earned the trust of the people. It is a mistake for a ruler to let those of superior virtue rank low, and it is a failure for him to let those of inferior virtue rank high. A ruler would rather mistreat a superior man than to misplace an inferior man.

6508

审其所好恶，则其长短可知也。观其交游，则其贤不肖可察也。

《管子·权修》

[英译]

Through investigation of what a person likes and what he dislikes, his defects and merits may be found. Through investigation of the friends he has made, it can be perceived whether or not he is a worthy.

6509

以天下之目视无不见也，以天下之耳听则无不闻也，以天下之心虑则无不知也。

《管子·九守》

[英译]

With the eyes of the people to watch, there is nothing that one fails to see. With their ears to listen, there is nothing that one fails to hear. With their minds to think, there is nothing that one fails to understand.

6510

不明于决塞，而欲驱众移民，犹使水逆流。

《管子·七法》

[英译]

If a ruler wants to drive people into action but does not have a clear mind about what to forbid and what to encourage, he will be no different from one who tries to make water flow upward.

6511

天不为一物枉其时，明君圣人亦不为一人枉其法。

《管子·白心》

[英译]

Heaven never varies the course of its seasons in favour of an individual living being, nor should a sage king break laws in favour of just one man.

6512

善人不能戚，恶人不能疏者危。

《晏子春秋·内篇问上》

[注释]

戚：亲近。

[英译]

One is in great jeopardy if one cannot be friendly to men of merit and keep a distance from men of evil.

6513

有贤而不知，一不详；知而不用，二不详；用而不仕，三不详。

《晏子春秋·内篇谏下》

[注释]

详：通“祥”。

[英译]

A ruler's first misfortune is failing to recognise the worthies though they are near to him. The second is failing to let these worthies display their excellence though he has recognised them. The third is failing to appoint them to key official posts though they have displayed their excellence.

6514

圣人常善救人，故人无弃人；常善救物，故物无弃物，是谓袭明。故善人者，不善人之师；不善人者，善人之资。

《老子》27章

[英译]

A sage always helps people to do their best. Thus there is not a single man left useless. He always helps other creatures to realise their full potential. Thus, there is not a single thing left useless. This is called taking advantage of the natural excellence. Therefore, a good man is the teacher of those who are not good and those who are not good are the material for the achievements of a good man.

6515

圣人去甚，去奢，去泰。

《老子》29章

［英译］

A sage avoids excess, extravagance, and the unachievable.

6516

圣人无常心，以百姓心为心。

《老子》49章

［英译］

A sage does not have a rigid mind. Instead, he takes the mind of the multitude as his own.

6517

江海所以能为百谷王者，以其善下之也。

《老子》66章

［英译］

The reason why the oceans and great rivers are superior to small rivers lies in the fact that they are good at choosing the lowest places.

6518

为政以德，譬如北辰，居其所，而众星共之。

《论语·为政》

［英译］

He who rules by means of virtues is like the pole-star, which remains in its place while all the lesser stars do homage to it.

6519

举直错诸枉，则民服；举枉错诸直，则民不服。

《论语·为政》

[注释]

错：废弃不用。

枉：不直。

[英译]

If a ruler promotes the straight but dismisses the crooked, his people will obey him. If, on the contrary, he promotes the crooked but dismisses the straight, his people will not obey him.

6520

政者正也，子帅以正，孰敢不正？

《论语·颜渊》

[英译]

Government means nothing but straightening. If the majority lead along a straight way, who will dare go by a crooked one?

6521

以不教民战，是谓弃之。

《论语·子路》

[英译]

To drive untrained people into military action only means sacrificing them.

6522

其身正,不令而行;其身不正,虽令不从。

《论语·子路》

[英译]

If a ruler himself leads along a strainght way, his policy will be successfully carried out by his people even though he does not command them. In contrast, if he cannot lead along a straight way himself, his policy will hardly be carried out even though he has commanded it.

6523

君子不以言举人,不以人废言。

《论语·卫灵公》

[英译]

A superior man does not promote persons only because of what they say, nor reject what they say only because the speakers are worthless.

6524

众恶之,必察焉;众好之,必察焉。

《论语·卫灵公》

[英译]

If something is disliked by all, it is indeed worth an investigation. If something is liked by all, it is indeed worth an investigation.

6525

子曰:“商,汝知君之为君乎?”子夏曰:“鱼失水则死,水失鱼犹为水也。”

《孔子集语·易者》

[英译]

Confucius questioned Zi Xia, a disciple of him, saying, "Do you know what the throne means for a king?" Zi Xia answered, "Without water, fish will die. Without fish, however, water remains water."

6526

政之急者,莫大乎使民富且寿也。

《孔子集语·贤君》

[英译]

The most urgent task for a government is to make the people rich and long-lived.

6527

仁人之所以为事者,必兴天下之利,除去天下之害,以此为事者也。

《墨子·兼爱中》

[英译]

The business of the benevolent is to promote advantages for the whole world and to remove disadvantages from the whole world. This is their only business.

6528

君子不求镜于水，而镜于人。镜于水，见面之容，镜于人，则知吉与凶。

《墨子·非攻中》

[英译]

Instead of still water, a gentleman will take other people as his mirror. Looking in the mirror of still water, he may see his own appearance only. Looking in the mirror of other people, he can foresee the fortune or misfortune he will meet.

6529

尚贤者，政之本也。

《墨子·尚贤上》

[英译]

The promotion of worthy people is the basis of government.

6530

有能则举之，无能则下之。

《墨子·尚贤上》

[英译]

Promote those who are talented and dismiss those who are worthless.

6531

政者，口言之，身必行之。

《墨子·公孟》

[英译]

Once a ruler talks about something，he must put it into action.

6532

国有贤良之士众，则国家之治厚；贤良之士寡，则国家之治薄。

《墨子·亲士》

[英译]

When a country possesses many worthy people，its government will be stable. If it possesses few，its government will be unstable.

6533

良弓难张，然可以及高入深；良马难乘，然可以任重致远。

《墨子·亲士》

[英译]

A good bow is difficult to bend，but it can reach targets higher and further than does a common bow. A good horse is difficult to ride，but it can carry heavier goods and gallop a greater distance.

6534

智者然后能知之，不可以为法，民不尽智；贤者而后知之，不可以为法，民不尽贤。故圣人之为法，必使之明白，易知，名正，愚知遍能知之。

《商君书·定分》

［英译］

Rules which can be understood only by the wise may not be taken as the rules of law because not all people are wise. Those which can be understood only by the worthies may not be taken as the rules of law because not all people are worthies. Therefore, sages, when making laws, must make them very clear and easy to understand, and properly defined, in order that both the stupid and the wise can understand them.

6535

圣人知必然之理，必为之时势。故为必治之政，战必勇之民，行必听之令。是以兵出而无敌，令行而天下服从。

《商君书·画策》

［英译］

A sage who can perceive the key principles among various theories and the underlying tendency among various developments can frame policies which are bound to lead to stability. He will fight against the enemy alongside people who are courageous, and issue the orders which need to be carried out. Therefore, when he initiates a military expedition, no enemy can resist him; when he issues an order, the whole world will obey him.

6536

庖有肥肉，厩有肥马，民有饥色，野有饿莩，此率兽而食人也。

《孟子·梁惠王上》

[**英译**]

If a ruler has fat meat in his kitchen and well-fed horses in his stables, while humans in the towns show hunger and those in rural areas die of starvation, he is causing animals to eat human beings.

6537

得道者多助，失道者寡助。寡助之至，亲戚畔之。多助之至，天下顺之。

《孟子·公孙丑下》

[**英译**]

One who has Tao will have many to support him. One who has not Tao will have few to help him. In extreme cases, the latter will find even his own relatives turning against him, while the former will have the whole world to obey him.

6538

入则无法家拂士，出则无敌国外患者，国恒亡。然后知生于忧患，死于安乐也。

《孟子·告子下》

[**注释**]

法家拂士：指坚持原则，敢于批评国君者。

[英译]

Without officers who are law-abiding and who dare to criticise their ruler within, without enemy countries as dangerous invaders outside, a state will inevitably come to an end. Then do we understand that life depends on anxieties and death results from ease and pleasure.

6539

大匠不为拙工改废绳墨,羿不为拙射变其彀率,君子引而不发,跃如也。中道而立,能者从之。

《孟子·尽心上》

[注释]

彀率:射箭的规矩。

[英译]

A great craftsman never changes or even puts aside his plumb-line for the benefit of a clumsy apprentice. Yi, a great master archer, never lowered his standards for the sake of clumsy archery. Similarly, a sage who is guiding and replacing his students, will persist in the Middle Way without compromise, and only those who are capable may follow him.

6540

贤者以其昭昭,使人昭昭;今以其昏昏,使人昭昭。

《孟子·尽心下》

[英译]

Of yore, the worthies enlightened others with their own enlightenment. Nowadays, however, many are trying to enlighten others with their own benighted ignorance.

6541

以德分人谓之圣人,以财分人谓之贤人。以贤临人,未有得人者也;以贤下人者,未有不得人者也。

《列子·力命》

[英译]

He who shares his brilliant virtues with others is called a sage; he who shares his wealth with others is called worthy. If a man looks down upon others, he can hardly have followers. If he behaves himself in a worthy way and is modest to others, he must have many followers.

6542

所谓四患者,好经大事,变更易常,以挂功名,谓之叨;专知擅事,侵人自用,谓之贪;见过不更,闻谏愈甚,谓之很;人同于己则可,不同于己,虽善不善,谓之矜。此四患也。

《庄子·渔父》

[英译]

People of the so-called "four troubles" are as follows: One who is fond of managing great affairs, and tries to obtain a reputation by constantly changing the rules and regulations is called ambitious; one who is conceited and autocratic, and forcing others to agree with and serve himself is greedy; one who never corrects his mistakes and becomes angry when they are pointed out is extreme; one who is friendly to whomever agrees with him and unkind to whomever disagrees with him is obstinate.

6543

非其事而事之,谓之摠;莫之顾而进之,谓之佞;希意道言,谓之谄;不择是非而言,谓之谀;好言人之恶,谓之谗;析交离亲,谓之贼;称誉诈伪以败恶人,谓之慝;不择善否,两容颊适,偷拔其所欲,谓之险。此八疵者,外以乱人,内以伤身,君子不友,明君不臣。

《庄子·渔父》

[注释]

摠:通"总",指到处插手。

两容:不分是非。

颊适:和颜媚色。

[英译]

Intervening in the business of others is meddling; giving advice without careful consideration is insensitive; speaking with the same mind as one's superior is obsequious; saying yes to whatever one's superior utters without discrimination between right and wrong is flattery; fond of denigrating others is slanderous; breaking off relations with friends and parents is scandalous; eulogizing others in a hypocritical way in order to ruin them is evil; looking always smooth and pleasant irrespective of good and bad happenings to realise one's own purpose in a secret way is insidious. These are the so-called "Eight Faults". With them, one is not only detrimental to others but endangering oneself also; and will be unable to make friends with superior men, or become a minister of intelligent kings.

6544

无过在于度数,无困在于豫备,慎在于畏小,智在于治大,除害在于敢断,得众在于下人。

《尉缭子·十二陵》

[英译]

It is rules and regulations that enable mankind to be immune from fault; it is elaborate preparations that enable him to be free from difficulties; it is the fear of even small dangers that enables him to be a cautious man; it is the excellent management of great affairs that enables him to be a man of wisdom; it is the resolution that enables him to get rid of troubles; it is the modesty towards those inferior to him that enables him to have support from the people.

6545

天下万事不可备能,责其备能于一人,则贤圣犹病诸。

《尹文子·大道上》

[英译]

Nothing in the world is capable of everything. If we look for a man who is capable of everything, even a sage is not qualified.

6546

昔齐桓好衣紫，阖境不鬻异彩；楚庄爱细腰，一国皆饥色。上之所以率下，乃治乱之所由也。

《尹文子·大道上》

［注释］

鬻：售。

［英译］

Of yore, the Duke Huan of Qi appreciated the colour purple only. As a result, there was no cloth of other colours for sale within his state. The King Zhuang of Chu appreciated slim beauties. As a result, the women all over his country looked hungry. Thus, once the superiors set an example, the inferiors will follow, and herein lies the line of demarcation between order and disorder.

6547

多言而类，圣人也。少言而法，君子也。多言无法，而流湎然，虽辩，小人也。

《荀子·大略》

［注释］

类：指近于道。

湎然：沉迷于酒。

［英译］

He who talks much and all that he says is identical with Tao is a sage. He who talks less and all that he says is in accordance with rules and regulations is a gentleman. He who talks much without rules and regulations and whose words are similar to those of a drunk is an inferior man, even though he might be quite eloquent.

6548

乐者，圣人之所乐也，而可以善民心，其感人深，其移风易俗，故先王尊之以礼乐而民和睦。

《荀子·乐论》

［英译］

Music is that with which the sages receive much pleasure, and it can improve people's minds by moving them deeply and transforming their habits. Therefore, the olden sage-kings encouraged ceremonies and music, and peace and harmony among the people were realised.

6549

君者，舟也；庶人者，水也。水则载舟，水则覆舟。

《荀子·哀公》

［英译］

The relationship between a king and the common people is similar to that between a boat and water. It is water on which a boat floats, and it is water on which the boat capsizes.

6550

主过一言而国残名辱，为后世笑。

《吕氏春秋·似顺》

［英译］

For a king, even one mistaken speech may ruin his country and bring humiliation upon himself, which will leave him ridiculous for later generations.

6551

令苛则不听,禁多则不行。

《吕氏春秋·吕货》

［英译］

Too many strict orders will not be carried out, and too many bans will have no effect.

6552

治国无法则乱,守法而弗变则悖,悖乱不可以持国。世易时移,变法宜矣。

《吕氏春秋·察今》

［英译］

To govern a country without laws and regulations leads to chaos while to stick to fixed laws without flexibility leads to irrational judgements. A country cannot survive with chaos and irrationality. With the shift of eras and passage of time, it is right to reform the laws.

6553

有术之君,不随适然之善,而行必然之道。

《韩非子·显学》

［英译］

A ruler with correct methods of government does not follow upon things which happened to bring about good results. Instead, he acts in accordance with Tao which is of certainty.

6554

圣人不期于修古，不法常可，论世之事，因为之备。宋人有耕田者，田中有株，兔走，触株折颈而死。因释其耒而守株，冀复得兔。兔不可复得，而身为宋国笑。今欲以先王之政，治当世之民，皆守株之类也。

《韩非子·五蠹》

［英译］

A sage neither seeks for following the ways of the ancients nor establishes any fixed standard for all times but examines the things of his age and then prepares to deal with them. There was in the State of Song a man, who tilled a field in which there stood a trunk of a tree. Once a hare rushed against the trunk, broke its neck, and died. Thereupon the man cast his plough aside and watched that tree, hoping that he would get other hares. Yet he never caught another one and was himself ridiculed by the people of Song. Those who are trying to govern the people of the present age with the policies of the former kings are doing the same as that man who watched the trunk of the tree.

6555

智术之士,必远见而明察,不明察不能烛私;能法之士,必强毅而劲直,不劲直不能矫奸。

《韩非子·孤愤》

[英译]

A wise man with correct methods of government must have far-reaching and sharp vision. Without sharp vision, he could not see through the machinations of selfish people. He who is talented and persists in laws must be unyielding and straightforward. Without being straightforward, he could not overcome evil.

6556

小信成则大信立,故明主积于信。赏罚不信,则禁令不行。

《韩非子·外储说左上》

[英译]

With trust set in a series of small things, great trust will be established. Therefore, an intelligent king pays attention to the accumulation of trusts. Without his rewards and punishment being trusted, his commands cannot be carried out.

6557

夫良药苦于口,而智者劝而饮之,知其入而已己疾也;忠言拂于耳,而明王听之,知其可以致功也。

《韩非子·外储说左上》

[英译]

Though bitter in taste, a wise man, when sick, will manage to take the good medicine because he knows that it can cure his disease. Though jarring on ears, an intelligent king will accept the criticism against him because he knows that it is helpful for him to achieve great success.

6558

毛羽不丰满者,不可以高飞;文章不成者,不可以诛罚;道德不厚者,不可以使民;政教不顺者,不可以烦大臣。

《战国策·秦策》

[英译]

Not yet full fledged, a bird cannot fly high in the sky; not yet renowned for cultural brilliance, a ruler cannot give out punishment; not yet well-cultivated morally, he cannot drive his people into action; not yet making government and education function properly, he cannot require his ministers to do difficult things.

6559

三人成虎,十夫楺椎,众口所移,毋翼而飞。

《战国策·秦策》

[注释]

楺椎:使直木弯曲。

[英译]

The rumour that a tiger had appeared in a downtown place would be believed if it is repeated by three persons. The rumour that a stick should be bent would be believed if it were reiterated by the people. Things are often distorted through the mouths of people and the rumours fly as fast as a bird though they do not have wings.

6560

见兔而顾犬,未为晚也;亡羊而补牢,未为迟也。

《战国策·楚策》

[英译]

It is not too late to summon a hound at the sight of a hare, and it is still in time to repair the sheepfold after some have strayed.

6561

以书为御者,不尽于马之情。以古制今者,不达于事之变。

《战国策·赵策》

[英译]

If one sticks to what is taught by books about horse-riding, one cannot well master equestrian skills. To govern the people today merely with the ancient knowledge of government, one cannot understand changes in the situation.

6562

礼世不必一其道,便国不必法古。圣人之兴也,不相袭而王。夏、殷之衰也,不易礼而灭。然则反古未可非,而循礼未足多也。

《战国策·赵策》

[注释]

礼世：当为"理世"，即治理国家。

[英译]

A ruler in his government does not necessarily keep a fixed way, nor should he necessarily imitate the rules and institutions set by the kings of antiquity, but do whatever benefits his country. When the ancient sages rose to govern the world, the later ones did not totally copy the earlier ones to attain true kingship. On the contrary, during the declining years of the Xia and Yin dynasties, the rulers did not change the rites and they came to ruin. From this we can learn that it is wrong to criticise something only because it is against ancient traditions, and that totally following the old rites is not praiseworthy.

6563

贤圣之君，不以禄私其亲，功多者授之；不以官随其爱，能当之者处之。故察能而授官者，成功之君也；论行而结交者，立名之士也。

《战国策·燕策》

[英译]

A wise king does not give handsome salaries to his relatives or those who are close to him, but to those who have the greatest achievements. He does not appoint those whom he loves to key posts but those who are capable. Therefore, he who appoints people to different posts in accordance with their capacities is a successful ruler; he who makes friends only with those who behave well is a promising gentleman.

6564

圣人之制事者，转祸而为福，因过而为功。

《战国策·燕策》

[英译]

When a sage governs, he always turns misfortunes into fortunes, and achieves success by taking lessons from failures.

6565

怨在不舍小过，患在不预定谋。福在积善，祸在积恶。饥在贱农，寒在惰织。安在得人，危在失事。富在迎来，贫在弃时。

《素书·安礼》

[英译]

It is when small faults are not forgiven that resentments arise; it is when consistent strategies are not well prepared that troubles come; it is through the accumulation of merit that luck befalls; it is through the accumulation of demerits that disasters befall; it is when agriculture is despised that there are famines; it is through the neglect of spinning and weaving that people die of cold; it is through having the right people governing that the country keeps stability and peace; it is through failures to act that a country is in jeopardy; it is through continuous diligence that one becomes rich;

it is through missing the right production cycle that one becomes poor.

6566

自疑不信人，自信不疑人。

《素书·安礼》

［英译］

He who is not resolute cannot trust others；he who has self-confidence will not harbour groundless suspicions against others.

6567

生之有时，而用之无节，则物力必屈。

《新书·无蓄》

［英译］

It takes time for living things to grow to maturity. If people do not consume them moderately，the material resources will inevitably be exhausted.

6568

前事不忘，后世之师也。

《新书·过秦论下》

［英译］

Do not forget previous experiences but take them as lessons for later generations.

6569

制国有常，利民为本；从政有经，令行为上。

《史记·赵世家》

[英译]

There is a constant principle in national government that benefiting the people should be considered the foundation. There is a changeless key in politics that the foremost need is to frame orders which can be carried out.

6570

忠言逆耳利于行，良药苦口利于病。

《史记·留侯世家》

[英译]

Though they may hurt ears, loyal criticism will lead to good effects. Though bitter in taste, good medicines are effective in curing illness.

6571

得人者兴，失人者崩。

《史记·商君列传》

[英译]

He who gets the support of the worthies will rise in politics; he who loses the support of them will come to ruin.

6572

文王拘而演周易，仲尼厄而作春秋，屈原放逐乃赋离骚，左丘失明厥有国语，孙子膑脚，兵法修列，不韦迁蜀，世传吕览，韩非囚秦，说难，孤愤，诗三百篇，大抵圣贤发愤之作为作也。

《报任安书》

[英译]

King Wen (of the Zhou Dynasty), when he was confined [by the tyrant Zhou (**纣王**) of the Shang Dynasty, before he took over the throne], developed the *Book of Changes* (**易经**). When (his political ideas were refused by the kings of the Warring States) and he felt frustrated, Confucius wrote the book *Spring and Autumn Annals* (**春秋**). Being exiled, Qu Yuan (**屈原**) composed *Li Sao* (**离骚**). Becoming blind, Zuo Qiu (**左丘**) completed *Guo Yu* (**国语**). After his knee-caps were chopped, Sun Wu (**孙武**) modified and published his book *Strategy and Tactics of War* (**孙子兵法**). After Lü Buwei (**吕不韦**) was exiled to Sichuan, he finished *Lü's Almanac* (**吕氏春秋**). Being imprisoned in the State of Qin, Han Fei (**韩非**) wrote his essays: *Shuo-Nan*, *Gu-Fen* (**说难，孤愤**). Most of the three hundred poems [in *The Book of Songs* (**诗经**)] were composed by saints when they were indignant at injustice.

6573

世不患不法，而患无必行之法也。

《盐铁论·申韩》

[英译]

The real worry of the world is not that we do not have enough laws and regulations but that the laws and regulations are not absolutely observed.

6574

十步之泽,必有香草;十室之邑,必有忠士。

《说苑·谈丛》

[英译]

Fragrant grass can be found in a marsh, even a small one; and at least one loyal man can be found within the smallest town.

6575

为国者,必先知民之所苦,祸之所起,然后设之以禁。

《潜夫论·述赦》

[英译]

A ruler of a country must first be conscious of the troubles of his people and know why disasters may befall. Then he is able to take measures to prevent them.

6576

用士不患其非国士,而患其非忠;世非患无臣,而患其非贤。

《潜夫论·论荣》

[英译]

When appointing an intellectual, what really needs to be worried about is not whether he is rated among the most talented of the country but whether he is loyal. And for a government, the real trouble is not that nobody is qualified to be a minister but that the ministers are not worthy.

6577

惟恤十难以任贤能，一曰不知，二曰不进，三曰不任，四曰不终，五曰小怨弃大德，六曰以小过黜大功，七曰以小失掩大美，八曰以奸讦伤忠正，九曰以邪说乱正度，十曰以谗嫉废贤能。是谓十难。十难不除，则贤臣不用，用臣不贤，则国非其国也。

《申鉴·政体》

［注释］

恤：忧虑。

讦：攻击别人短处。

［英译］

Problems for the promotion of the worthy and talented are the following ten difficulties: The first is the ruler's ignorance of them; the second is the lack of people to recommend them; the third is failure to appoint them; the fourth is inconsistency in treating them; the fifth is the negation of their great virtues because of small private resentments; the sixth is denial of their great achievements because of their small faults; the seventh is obliteration of their great merits because of their small defects; the eighth is perverse criticisms against loyal and just people; the ninth is confusion of right rules and regulations caused by heterodox theories; and the tenth is slander against the worthy and talented. These are called "ten difficulties". Without overcoming them, those who are worthy cannot be appointed to key posts and those who are appointed to the key posts cannot be worthy. If such is the case, a country cannot long survive.

6578

伪乱俗,私坏法,放越轨,奢败制。四者不除,则政未由行矣。

《申鉴·政体》

[英译]

Hypocrisy disrupts customs; selfishness ruins legal systems; dissoluteness transgresses moral standards; extravagance destroys institutions. Unless these four evils are removed, there is no way to have a good government.

6579

善禁者,先禁其身而后人。不善禁者,先禁人而后身。善禁之至于不禁,令亦如之。若乃肆情于身,而绳欲于众,行诈于官,而矜实于民,求己之所有余,夺下之所不足,舍己之所易,责人之所难,怨之本也。

《申鉴·政体》

[注释]

矜实:慎重求实。

[英译]

He who is good at laying down laws will observe them first; he who is not good at keeping the law will require others to observe it first and then extend it to himself. Thus the best prohibition is not issued by force [but works well through the example of the ruler himself]. The same applies to commands. If a ruler is undisciplined himself and satisfies his own sensual needs while depressing the desires of the people; if his court is full of hypocrits, while he expects other to be honest; if he accumulates wealth by robbing the poor; if he treats himself leniently while driving others to accomplish difficult tasks; he is in fact digging a grave for himself.

6580

凡物穷则思变,困则谋通。

王弼《周易·困卦注》

[英译]

Changes will take place when things come to a dead end, and breakthroughs can be expected when there is no way out.

6581

无私于天下,则天下之风一也。

郭象《庄子注·则阳》

[英译]

If a ruler does not have personal preferences for anything at all, the diversity in customs will disappear.

6582

世有雷同之誉，而未必贤也。俗有讙哗之毁，而未必恶也。是以迎而许之者，未若鉴其事而诚其用。逆而距之者，未若听其言而课其实。则佞媚不以虚谈进，良能不以孤弱退。

《抱朴子·广譬》

［**注释**］

讙哗：即“喧哗”。

［**英译**］

Those who are unanimously praised are not necessarily worthy people. Those who receive a great deal of criticisms are not necessarily evil persons. Therefore, it is better for a ruler to examine a man's previous deeds and to make certain of his capacity through practice rather than to appoint him to the key post as soon as a widely praised man is found; it is better to listen to his speech and to look into his real nature than to keep him at a distance when a widely criticised man is found. In so doing, the cunning and evil persons will not be promoted through empty talk, and the men of real capacity will not be dismissed because they appear isolated and weak.

6583

贵远而贱近者，常人之用情也。信耳而疑目者，古今之所患也。

《抱朴子·广譬》

［**英译**］

It is a common prejudice of ordinary folk to exalt things that are afar while belittling things near, and it is a common trouble throughout history to believe what is heard while suspecting what is seen.

6584

官达者才未必当其位，誉美者实未必负其名。

《抱朴子·博喻》

[英译]

Those who have high rank are not necessarily worthy of their posts; those who receive lofty praise are not necessarily praiseworthy.

6585

狱者，人命之所悬也，不可以不慎。贤人君子，国家之基也，不可以不敬。稼穑者，国之本也，不可以不急。酒色便佞，乱德之甚也，不可以不戒。

《晋书·慕容廆载记》

[英译]

A trial is a matter of life and death, and hence caution is needed. Worthy people and noble men are the basis of a country, and hence respect to them is needed. Agriculture is the foundation of a country, and hence priority need to be given to it. Indulgence in wine, women and flattery are the worst immoralities, and hence they need to be prevented.

6586

大器不可小用，小器不可大用。

萧绎《金楼子·杂记》

［英译］

Men of great capacity cannot be asked to deal with trivial matters whereas men of small capacity cannot be trusted to do important tasks.

6587

车摧轮则无以行，舟无楫则无以济，国之乏贤则无以理。

《刘子·荐贤》

［英译］

With broken wheels a carriage cannot move an inch; with oars lost, a boat cannot cross a river; with lack of worthy people, a country cannot have a good government.

6588

夫桎柏之断也，大者为之栋梁，小者为之椽桁，直者中绳，曲者中钩，随材而适，未有可弃者。是以君子善能拔士，故无弃人。

《刘子·适才》

［注释］

桁：梁上的横木。

［英译］

When trees are felled, the big ones will be taken as ridgepoles; the small ones, rafters; the straight timbers, straight articles; the bent branches, curved articles. All are utilised according to their different qualities without any rejects. Similarly, a skilful ruler will promote talented people according to their different capabilities, leaving no one unused.

6589

俗之观士者,见其威仪屑屑,好行细洁,乃谓英彦。士有大趣,不修容议,不惜小检,而谓之弃人。是见朱桔一子蠹,因剪树而弃之;睹缛锦一寸点,乃全疋而燔之。

《刘子·妄瑕》

[注释]

屑屑:烦细貌。

[英译]

Ordinary folk tend to judge an intellectual in such a way that they will call him a real genius if he bothers greatly about his appearance and pays much attention to trivial matters; and they will call him useless if he solely aspires to great things, not caring about his appearance nor trivial things. In so doing, these folk are not acting any differently than cutting down an orange tree just because one of its fruits is worm-eaten or burning a whole bolt of silk only because the material has one flaw.

6590

克简节用,实弘道之源;崇侈恣情,乃败德之本。

吴兢《贞观政要》

［英译］

Frugality is a source of the prosperity of Tao, and extravagance and indulgence are the basis of moral decline.

6591

以铜为镜,可以正衣冠;以古为镜,可以知兴替;以人为镜,可以明得失。

吴兢《贞观政要》

［英译］

With polished metal as a mirror, one's appearance can be made trim; with history as a mirror, vicissitude of society can be known; with others as a mirror, right and wrong can be clearly understood.

6592

圣人一视而同仁,笃近而举远。

韩愈《原人》

［英译］

The sages treat people equally without discrimination, and they benefit people close to them and recommend those afar.

6593

天下虽兴,好战必亡;天下虽安,忘战必危;不好不忘,天下之王也。

白居易《白居易集·议兵策》

[英译]

Though a country is now prosperous, bellicosity will surely lead to its ruin; though a country is now peaceful, neglect of military affairs will surely endanger it. Only when a ruler is neither bellicose nor negligent of military affairs, can he achieve the kingship over all under Heaven.

6594

敌存灭祸,敌去招过。

柳宗元《敌戒》

[英译]

A country which doesn't have an enemy without may have civil unrest within, and vice versa.

6595

非药曷以愈疾?非兵胡以定乱?

柳宗元《愈膏肓疾赋》

[英译]

Without medicines, how could diseases be cured? Without an army, how could rebellions be put down?

6596

灭六国者,六国也,非秦也。族秦者,秦也,非天下也。

杜牧《阿房宫赋》

[英译]

The six Warring States perished by themselves, not by the State of Qin. Similarly, the Qin Dynasty perished by itself, not by the people under Heaven.

6597

历览前贤国与家，成由勤俭败由奢。

《李义山集·咏史》

［英译］

Thorough reflection on the historic experiences of state government as well as on family management tells us that frugality leads to prosperity while extravagance leads to destruction.

6598

省事不如省官，省官不如省吏，能简冗官，诚治本也。

《新唐书》

［英译］

To streamline state affairs is no better than to simplify administration, and to simplify administration is no better than to reduce the number of officers. To cut out useless posts is indeed the basis of a good government.

6599

得士者昌，失士者亡。

范仲淹《文集》

［英译］

With first-class intellectuals, a country is rising; without them, it is declining.

6600

先天下之忧而忧,后天下之乐而乐。

《岳阳楼记》

［英译］

A leader should worry before all the people are worried and be delighted after the delight of all the people.

6601

礼义治人之大法,廉耻立人之大节。盖不廉则无所不取,不耻则无所不为,人而如此,则祸败乱亡,亦无所不至。况为大臣而无所不取,无所不为,则天下其有不乱,国家岂有不亡者乎?

欧阳修《冯道传》

［英译］

Rites and righteousness are the fundamental principles for the management of people whereas honesty and dignity are the fundamental requirements for the education of people. Without honesty, one will accept all things no matter whether or not one should take them. Without dignity, one will do whatever one intends no matter whether or not they are proper and righteous. If such a man is an ordinary person, he will suffer disasters, failures, disorders and death, which come inevitably. If he is a chief minster, it will be impossible during his time to keep stability and for his country to survive.

6602

夫为人主者，非欲养祸于内而疏忠臣硕士于外，盖其渐积而势使之然也。

欧阳修《五代史宦者传论》

［英译］

Any ruler would not keep traitors inside his government and keep loyal officials and learned scholars away from his government. However, gradual accumulation of mistakes would force him to do what he would not do.

6603

忧劳可以兴国，逸豫可以亡身，自然之理也。

欧阳修《伶官传序》

［英译］

It is natural that worries and toil lead to the rise of a country, whereas ease and complacency may lead to one's doom.

6604

夫国以一人兴，以一人亡。贤者不悲其身之死，而忧其国之衰，故必复有贤者，而后可以死。

苏洵《管仲论》

［英译］

There are cases when a country rises only because of the existence of an outstanding individual, and when a country is ruined only because of the lack of such a person. Thus when dying, a worthy person will not worry about the end of his life but the decline of his country. Only when another worthy person has been found to replace him can he die satisfied.

6605

夫天下未尝无贤者,盖有有臣而无君者矣。

苏洵《管仲论》

[英译]

There has never been a case throughout history when no worthy person can be found in a country. However, there have been many cases when kings have failed to recognise the worthy people and to appoint them to key posts.

6606

人之慕名,如水之趋下,上有所好,下必甚焉。

《资治通鉴》

[英译]

Running after reputation is a natural tendency of men, similar to the fact that water flows down hill. Thus, as soon as a ruler shows preference for something, his subjects will appreciate it with extraordinary zeal.

6607

取其道不取其人，务其实不务其名。

《资治通鉴》

［英译］

Judge a person through the Tao he follows instead of his personal character; pay attention to the reality of things instead of their names.

6608

才盛于德，谓之小人；德盛于才，谓之君子；德才兼备，谓之圣人。

《资治通鉴》

［英译］

He whose talents exceed his virtues is called an inferior man; he whose virtues exceed his telents is called a superior man; he who has both brilliant virtues and great talents is called a sage.

6609

民可明也，不可愚也；民可教也，不可威也；民可顺也，不可强也；民可使也，不可欺也。

《二程集》

［英译］

People can be enlightened but not fooled; they can be taught but not threatened; they can be guided but not forced to do things; they can be ordered but not cheated.

6610

天下之患，莫大于不知其然而然。不知其然而然者，是拱手而待乱也。

苏轼《策略》

[英译]

No trouble of the world is greater than to do things without knowing the right way to do it. If one does things without knowing the right way to do them, one is waiting for chaos with helpless hands.

6611

物必先腐也，而后虫生之；人必先疑也，而后谗入之。

苏轼《范增论》

[英译]

Worms will grow in something if it is already rotten. Gossip will rise, only if it causes suspicion.

6612

天下之事，常成于困约，而败于奢靡。

陆游《放翁家训》

[注释]

约：贫困。

[英译]

Affairs of the world are usually well accomplished through toil and hardship, and they are usually ruined through extravagance and luxury.

6613

贤路当广而不当狭，言路当开而不当塞。

《宋史·乔行简传》

［英译］

A government should be wide open to men of various talents as well as to different opinions and suggestions.

6614

虑天下者，常图其所难，而忽其所易；备其所可畏，而遗其所不疑。然祸常发于所忽之中，而乱常起于不足疑之事。

方孝孺《深虑论》

［英译］

A ruler who is concerned with the whole world often considers difficult matters while neglecting the easy ones; he often makes sufficient preparation against the most dangerous things while failing to think over the seemingly indubitable ones. However, disasters often take place in the matters he neglects and disorders often begin with indubitable matters.

6615

大其心，容天下之物；虚其心，受天下之善；平其心，受天下之事；潜其心，观天下之理；定其心，应天下之意。

吕坤《呻吟语》

［英译］

Widen your mind so that it can contain all the things in the world; empty your mind so that it can accept all the goodness of the world; calm your mind so that it can tolerate all happenings of the world; deepen your mind so that it can find out all principles of the world; concentrate your mind so that it can meet all the needs of the world.

6616

不以一己之利为利，而使天下受其利；不以一己之害为害，而使天下释其害。

黄宗羲《明夷待访录·原君》

[英译]

Do not consider your own benefits as real benefits, but try to benefit the whole world; do not consider the harm that comes to you as real harm, but try to remove the harms of the whole world.

6617

天下风俗最坏之地，清议尚存，犹足以维持一二；至于清议亡，则干戈至矣。

顾炎武《日知录·清议》

[英译]

Even the government of a most corrupt country may survive for a time if it allows ordinary people to criticise it. As soon as such criticism is banned, disasters of war will befall.

6618

士皆知有耻，则国家永无耻矣；士不知耻，为国之大耻。

龚自珍《明良论》

[英译]

If all the gentlemen of a country have a sense of dignity, their country will no longer suffer indignities. If they do not have a sense of dignity, that itself is the greatest indignity the country suffers.

6619

师夷长技以制夷。

魏源《海国图志·筹海篇》

[英译]

Learn the most advanced techniques from the barbarian countries in order to tame them.

6620

不知人之短，不知人之长，不知人长中之短，不知人短中之长，则不可以用人，不可以教人。用人者，取人之长，辟人之短；教人者，成人之长，去人之短也。惟尽知己之所短而后能去人之短，惟不恃己之所长而后能收人之长。不然，但取己所明而已，但取己所近而已。

《魏源集·默觚下》

[英译]

Someone who does not know the shortcomings of other people,

their strong points, their shortcomings hidden behind strong points, and their strong points covered by shortcomings, can neither be a ruler who properly appoints people to posts nor a teacher who correctly instructs people. To appoint people properly, a ruler should let their strong points be fully displayed while avoiding the effects of shortcomings. To teach people, a teacher should accentuate their strong points while removing their shortcomings. Only when one knows one's own shortcomings can one remove the shortcomings of others. Only when one does not consider only one's own point of view can one accept people in considering their strong points. Otherwise, a ruler will only accept opinions similar to his own and accept solely the people close to him.

6621

世昌则言昌,言昌则才愈昌;世幽则言幽,言幽则才愈幽。

《魏源集·默觚下》

[英译]

A prosperous time brings about a prosperity of opinions, and a prosperity of opinions stimulates the appearance of talented people. On the contrary, a dark time brings about a shortage of opinions, and a shortage of opinions suppresses talented people.

《先哲名言》索引

责任编辑　蔡希勤
封面设计　张大羽

图书在版编目(CIP)数据

先哲名言＝CHINESE MAXIMS：汉英对照/宫达非，冯禹主编。—北京：华语教学出版社，1994.9

ISBN 7－80052－424－8/H・492(外)

I. 先…　II. ①宫…　②冯…　III. 格言－中国－汇编－汉、英　IV. H136.3

中国版本图书馆 CIP 数据核字(94)第 06984 号

先哲名言

*

华语教学出版社出版
(中国北京百万庄路 24 号)
邮政编码 100037
北京外文印刷厂印刷
中国国际图书贸易总公司发行
(中国北京车公庄西路 35 号)
北京邮政信箱第 399 号　邮政编码 100044
1994 年 (大 32 开) 第一版
1996 年第二次印刷
(汉英)
01970
9－CE－2916P